Pak Proxy War

Pak Proxy War

A Story of ISI, bin Laden and Kargil

Rajeev Sharma

Foreword by

Air Chief Marshal (Retd) N C Suri

2002

Kaveri Books

New Delhi - 110 002

First Published in 1999
Second Impression 2002

ISBN 81-7479- 035-7

Published by : **Kaveri Books**
21-A, Ansari Road,
New Delhi - 110 002 (India)
Tel.: 328 8140, 324 5799 Fax: 011 719 9029
E-mail: kaveribooks@vsnl.com

Printed at : Chawla Printers, Delhi - 110 052.

PRINTED IN INDIA

Dedicated to the memory of my late mother, Mrs Ratan Sharma and my late father, Dr Rattan Lal Sharma, whose sudden death in August 1998 has made me feel that this life is a long, painful sleepwalk.

ACKNOWLEDGEMENTS

I am thankful to :

* My wife, Dr Pratima and sister, Sarika, whose sustained cooperation enabled me to complete this book. Pratima has been patience incarnated as I neglected her, and our son, Himank, for months.
* My journalist friends, Mr Jayant Ghoshal of Bengali daily *Bartaman* and Mr Kamal Kant Gauri of *"Rajasthan Patrika"* for giving their valuable suggestions.
* Mr T R Ramachandran, Political Editor of *Newstime-Eenadu*, for his help and co-operation.
* My uncles, Mr Jagdish Chaturvedi and Dr Kamal Kishore Goenka, who encouraged me a lot to write this book.
* My several sources in different agencies who made available to me a lot of important material but wish to remain anonymous.
* The publisher, Mr Rakesh Goel, whose unstinted cooperation made the publication of this book possible.

Rajeev Sharma

FOREWORD

I have known Rajeev Sharma in his capacity as a journalist specialising earlier in Defence issues and later in international security and investigation-related matters. My happiness in writing this Foreword has been accentuated not only by the fact that he has a very incisive mind and an ability to articulate with passion and conviction, but also as he is possibly the first Indian author who has attempted to write on the notorious Pakistani intelligence agency, called the ISI.

This book covers a wide canvas in respect of proxy wars and brings to the forefront the need for the civilised world to act in concert in eradicating the uncivilised and uncouth acts of terrorism. In a wider sense, it is my belief that the views expressed by the author have a far deeper connotation than merely enunciating the ills of terrorism in a civilised society. I believe that it is sacrilegious that anyone or any group of people can incite or spread mayhem, brutality and act of hatred in the name of religion. No religion in the world advocates such acts which are inhuman or uncivilised. In fact, religion, apart from being a personal matter, creates a link between man and God and under no circumstances either distances man from God or man from man. It is in this context that we have to take a very serious look at a group of people who are determined on destroying the world that we live in. These people are basically mercenaries and their motivations are decidedly not religious.

This book — "Pak Proxy War : A Story of ISI, Bin Laden and Kargil"— gives an insight into the grave dangers that lie ahead of us, which if not curbed in a timely fashion, may eventually lead us to a point of no return in terms of terrorism. Pakistan, unfortunately, has now attained the unique distinction of being a terrorist state and a rogue country. It is unfortunate that hitherto the Western world with its somewhat limited vision has fuelled the fire and inadvertently promoted countries like Pakistan in its acts of terrorism.

Apart from the USA and India which have openly been threatened by Osama bin Laden as his primary targets, Russia feels equally threatened in its Muslim areas of Dagestan, Tatarstan, Bashkiria, Ingushetia and North Ossetia. Similarly, China appears to be just as worried in respect of its own Muslim predominant areas.

Today, we have Osama bin Laden, a Saudi Arabian billionaire, promoting and exciting the movement of terrorism on a global scale. Eliminating him is no guarantee of eliminating acts of terrorism in the world as after him many more such bin Ladens will resurrect. So to put an end to this barbarism, the civilised world must join hands and stand by their moral obligations to fellow human beings. In our immediate neighbourhood, Pakistan is a feudal society governed not merely by the political party power, but by the militants, the clergy, the unprincipled army and the unethical ISI.

Pakistan's interest in promoting terrorism seems to stem from the fact that there is nothing which can even remotely be called indigenous or Pakistani that they can boast of since Independence in August 1947. In fact, their's is a problem of crisis in identity and the only way that they feel could help them to be known in the world is through promotion of acts of terrorism. Sadly, the terrorism with which they threaten their neighbour is also not indigenous but imported from other like-minded countries.

India must no longer cajole Pakistan but act with firmness and with the language that they best understand. While we do not have to be Pakistan-centric, we must not allow Pakistan to interpret our patience as a sign of weakness. Experience has shown that in dealing with them we can no longer remain reactive but must now become pro-active and prevent them from continuing to be of nuisance value.

The democracies of the world must now get together without further loss of time and devise ways and means of ensuring a better tomorrow for those who cherish values. This is particularly so as there is no other world forum which can be depended upon to promote peace and harmony and eradicating wrong doing. The United Nations which was created 54 years ago after 53 million people died in the World War, today lies not not only dormant but totally powerless and impotent. The reading of this book by the intelligentsia, and particularly the departments of the government dealing with national security and defence, would be prudent as it gives food for thought which could help us come to grips with the reality of the demon of terrorism.

Air Chief Marshal (Retd) N C Suri*

---

* Suri was the Chief of Indian Air Force from 1991 to 1993. During his 44-year-long distinguished service in the IAF, he climbed up the ladder to occupy the highest post after having worked on key positions, including Air Officer Commanding-in-Chief and Vice-Chief of Air Staff. Currently, he is on the Board of Directors of several Companies.

CONTENTS

Preface

Kargil did not happen overnight. It was a result of Pakistan's increasing audacity over the years which largely flowed from India's unwillingness to take the bull by its horns and give a befitting military response.

The climate for launching the Kargil operation was prepared by the ever-increasing terrorist and subversive activities unleashed by ISI against India since the late seventies. By the year 1999, the Pakistani strategists became so bold that for the first time Pakistan Army was involved in the ongoing proxy war. Not content with this, Pakistani authorities had the cheek to threaten a country of one billion people of "more Kargils".

A remarkable thing is that Pakistan has never faced a resource crunch for its anti-India operations, though the Pakistani economy is in tatters, particularly after Islamabad announced its nuclear status. It is an open secret that the ISI and other government arms of Pakistan, have been indulging in massive drug-trafficking operations to finance their not-so-secret operations against India. Pakistan accounts for a whopping ten per cent of the global narcotic market, estimated to be worth three trillion dollars annually.

The Kargil developments marked another watershed : the involvement of fugitive Saudi billionnaire, Osama bin Laden, and his Islamist band of Afghan Mujahideen in the 'jehad' in Kashmir. Now that the Talibanisation of Pakistan is complete,

India, with more Muslims than in Pakistan, is the new target country for the Taliban.

Against this backdrop, this book attempts to give comprehensive details on the ISI, bin Laden, Taliban, Pakistan Army, the SSG and Pakistan's neck-deep involvement in drug-trafficking. A combination of all these factors led to the Kargil incursions.

The bin Laden angle is important because the Saudi fanatic has successfully challenged and defeated one superpower in Afghanistan and is so far successful in taking on another. The fact that the exploits of bin Laden in Afghanistan and other Islamic countries have made him a living legend is a cause of concern for India as well as the United States.

In fact, New Delhi and Washington were never so close as they are today, mainly because of the bin Laden factor. There is a more urgent need for India and the US to work jointly to tackle the menace represented by this pivotal figure of pan-Islamic activities.

This book seeks to detail the circumstances and the various acts of omission and commission of Islamabad which warrant the US and other Western powers to declare Pakistan a terrorist state.

For last two decades, India has had to contend with a rogue secret service called ISI. Kargil developments have added a more sinister dimension. Now India has to face Pakistan Army as well—not in a war theater but in an ISI-type proxy war situation.

Pakistan has come a long way in past two decades. From a hesitant collusion with Punjab extremists in the late seventies, to a brazen, full-scale arms training of not just Punjab ultras but dozens of militant outfits in Jammu and Kashmir, north-east and other parts of India, the tentacles of the ISI octopus grew longer and longer. For reasons unknown, governments after governments in New Delhi failed to take a strong and effective action against Pakistan. They only mouthed 'warnings' and 'ultimatums'.

New Delhi's conduct has been mostly reactive — reacting to Pakistani provocative acts, within India. When Atal Behari Vajpayee government came to power in 1998, Home Minister L K Advani announced that he would be pursuing a "pro-active" policy vis-a-vis Pakistan. This comment raised a furore and opposition political parties accused Advani of taking a hawkish stand. But even Advani and his government failed to give a befitting reply to Pakistan when Islamabad's audacity crossed all limits with the Kargil incursions. India did not cross the Line of Control even then.

When Pakistan shot down an Indian fighter aircraft and killed in cold blood its pilot, Squadron Leader Ajay Ahuja, India showed 'exemplary restraint'. When the mutilated bodies of six Indian soldiers, who were tortured to death during captivity in Pakistan, arrived back, New Delhi still did not cross the LoC. None asked what happened to Advani's pro-active doctrine.

All this points to the Indian malaise of the so-called tolerance. Malaise because when tolerance is exercised even in the face of most serious provocations, it is interpreted for weakness or lack of will power to act decisively. National security is not the responsibility of the government alone. Opposition parties are equally responsible in a vibrant democracy like India. But unfortunately, till date, no opposition party has specifically called for carrying out armed raids and destroying the more than one hundred terrorist training camps being run in Pakistan Occupied Kashmir (POK) and Afghanistan.

Opposition parties must understand that by making a clamour for such pre-emptive strikes, they would not only be exerting pressure on the Central Government to act decisively vis-a-vis Pakistan, they would also be forcing the rogue state called Pakistan to stop in its tracks and think that the 'more Kargils' threat could result in more Bangladeshs.

RAJEEV SHARMA

September 1999, New Delhi

PART I

KARGIL

1 The Intrusion

On May 9, 1999, Prime Minister Atal Behari Vajpayee was sitting in his office chamber at his 7, Race Course Road residence. He was in a cheerful mood. Suddenly his RAX phone rang. George Fernandes was on the line. The conversation lasted a few minutes. His mood changed within minutes as he listened intently to his Defence Minister.

Vajpayee hung up after a few minutes, but not before telling Fernandes to immediately come over to him.

Vajpayee told the caller that it was a "dangerous development". Fernandes had just informed him that Pakistani Army regulars and militants had entrenched themselves deep inside the Indian territory in the Kargil sector. Fernandes named Dras, Batalik and Kargil as the areas of Pakistani incursion—the names which were to become household geographical locations just a few days later.

Vajpayee sat speechless, motionless for about five minutes after he hung up. Obviously, his thoughts were drifting to his much-publicised Lahore bus diplomacy in February. His Pakistani counterpart, Nawaz Sharif, was then all sugar and honey. But the information Fernandes had just given was explosive and showed the other side of Sharif.

After some time, he directed his Private Secretary Shakti Sinha to immediately call up Union Home Minister L K Advani and National Security Advisor Brajesh Mishra to rush to 7, RCR.

External Affairs Minister Jaswant Singh, one of the most trustworthy Ministers of Vajpayee, was in Russia at this point of time on a pre-scheduled visit. Vajpayee rang up Singh and informed him about the Kargil developments. The Prime Minister asked Singh to come back as early as possible. Singh could not agree more.

Within fifteen minutes, the three summoned persons had assembled at 7, RCR for what transpired to be a brainstorming session which lasted for about an hour.

Fernandes gave further details of the Pakistani incursion in Kargil sector. Everybody put a volley of questions to the Defence Minister. Fernandes could barely complete a sentence without getting interjected, now by PM, then by Advani and then by Mishra.

Fernandes was clearly at the receiving end at this hastily convened meeting. He pointed out that he had been getting "contradictory" reports as to when the intrusion took place. While some reports had suggested that the incursion took place in April, some other reports suggested that it occurred in May itself. This was being verified.

What Fernandes did tell was that Army jawans deployed in Batalik cantonment had spotted on May 6 some bearded Pathan-like strongly-built men dressed in black. Obviously these men were foreigners. The jawans, while routinely scouring the Line of Control through powerful telescopes, had noticed the presence of the intruders.

The next day, a reconnaissance plane made a sortie over the areas of suspected intrusion. The inevitable happened. The heavily-armed intruders attacked the plane with anti-aircraft guns. The plane was damaged but it managed to return to its base safely.

Advani said in a grim mood that several alert messages and reports had been coming from intelligence agencies and the Border Security Force (BSF), warning of the developments in Kargil sector. These messages had started coming from December itself. But then he hastily added, and everybody nodded in agreement, that this was not the time for probing what went wrong, where and when. Time had come for action.

The Kargil crisis had erupted

Vajpayee was in a piquant situation. The BJP-led coalition government headed by him had been voted out of power by one single vote in March. He and his Cabinet colleagues, particularly his trouble-shooter Defence Minister, had remained bogged down for months in an equally fierce political war with the estranged ally, Jayalalitha. It was a war of political survival which the Vajpayee government had lost.

But this time, a different war was glaring in his face. The threat this time had come from across the border and the nation's unity and integrity was in peril like never before since 1971. And Vajpayee did not want to lose this war.

Islamabad had carefully played its political chess game. Nawaz Sharif had lulled the Indians into complacency with the Lahore Declaration. Vajpayee had seized the initiative for improving ties with a hostile neighbour—a neighbour which has been waging a proxy war against India for the past two decades.

Vajpayee had responded to a suggestion from Sharif that why could not the Indian Prime Minister board the inaugural Delhi-Lahore bus which was scheduled in the next couple of weeks. Sharif had given this suggestion in an interview to *Indian Express* Editor, Shekhar Gupta. Sharif had also stated that he would go back with Vajpayee to India in the same bus and the Indo-Pak differences would thus be sunk in a jiffy.

Vajpayee did board the bus to Lahore. Sharif never accompanied Vajpayee back to India. What happened in Lahore was indicative of the things to come.

Pakistan Army Chief General Pervez Musharraf, the main protagonist of the Kargil misadventure, and the Chiefs of Pakistani Air Force and Navy were conspicuous by their absence when Vajpayee had crossed into Wagah. This was inexplicable then. It was against the protocol that the Pakistani Prime Minister is going to Wagah to receive the Indian Prime Minister on the

Attari-Wagah land border and the three Services Chiefs were not present. The subsequent developments later demonstrated why the Pakistani Services Chiefs did not turn up to receive Vajpayee.

The Pakistani military was clearly against talking peace with Vajpayee. A meeting of Pakistan's Cabinet Committee of Defence was held a few days before Vajpayee's scheduled visit. The meet was stormy. Musharraf said without mincing words that he could not salute the Prime Minister of an "enemy" country.

The mood in Pakistan was clear.

Musharraf had to call on Vajpayee in the Governor's House at Lahore. There he shook hands with Vajpayee but did not salute.

Despite these not-so-subtle signals, the Vajpayee government believed in Sharif's words. The army patrolling on the Line of Control, particularly in the Kargil Sector, was reduced as the government presumed that after the Lahore Declaration the patrolling expenses could be avoided.

On May 10, a Sunday, by when the Indian Army had started skirmishes with the intruders, Vajpayee rang up Nawaz Sharif. The Indian Premier told his Pakistani counterpart that the Pakistani act was nothing but a great betrayal, particularly when it came barely two and a half months after they had talked peace.

Sharif feigned total ignorance of whatever was happening in Kargil. Vajpayee briefed his Cabinet about the conversation he had with Sharif the same day and also instructed the intelligence agencies to find out whether Sharif's claim that he was not aware of the Kargil intrusion was correct or not. Subsequent developments called Sharif's bluff.

From then on, the Vajpayee government devoted its entire time and energy on the Kargil developments only. The Cabinet Committee on Security (CCS) held meetings virtually every day, sometimes even twice a day. The CCS meetings were chaired by Vajpayee. Others who attended the CCS meetings were Advani, Fernandes, Jaswant Singh, Brajesh Mishra and Finance Minister

Yashwant Sinha. The three Service Chiefs-- Army Chief Gen V P Malik, Air Chief A Y Tipnis and Naval Chief Admiral Sushil Kumar invariably attended these meetings.

Quite often the political leadership got together and held discussions before the Services Chiefs were called. This used to happen when they had to discuss highly contentious issues. The idea was to avoid having heated discussions and division among top ministers in front of the Services Chiefs. The induction of Indian Air Force (IAF) in the Kargil operations was one such contentious issue.

By mid-May, it had become clear that the Indian Army was up against no ordinary intruders. The intruders were using sophisticated weapons, were entrenched in well-fortified positions on commanding heights of the glaciated region, and were getting reinforcements of logistics from across the border. It was going to be a long and bloody operation to drive out the intruders. By that time, it was not known that it was the Pakistan Army soldiers with a sprinkling of Mujahideen and not the other way round as was believed then.

At one of the CCS meetings, Gen Malik likened the situation to the Indian Army jawans trying to crawl up the Qutab Minar in the face of heavy gun fire from the enemy entrenched firmly on the top. The Army Chief argued that it was an unequal war and the number of Indian casualties was mounting alarmingly. He said it was not upto the Indian Army alone to flush out these heavily-armed intruders who were commanding strategic heights. Therefore, Gen Malik argued, the IAF had to be inducted into the Kargil war zone

Air Chief Marshal A Y Tipnis vociferously opposed Gen Malik's plea, saying that the use of air force would inevitably be escalatory and could lead to a full-scale war with Pakistan. The Air Chief asked a million-dollar question : is India prepared for a war with Pakistan and, if yes, have all the necessary war mobilisation measures been taken ?

The Air Chief's argument was followed by long moments of tension-filled silence. This issue was to be debated at the subsequent CCS meetings over the next few days.

Then started a massive war mobilisation effort. The three Strike Corps of the Indian Army were pulled out of the barracks and deployed strategically. All the base hospitals of the three Services were geared up for a war. Extra beds were put. Stocks of life saving drugs were beefed up. Arrangements were made for arranging the necessary medical and para-medical staff at these hospitals in anticipation of heavy casualties.

All the forward bases of the IAF were put on alert. The three Services quickly beefed up their POL (Petroleum, Oil and Liquefied Gas) reserves which could last them for at least a month. Sizable POL reserves were moved to strategic locations.

POL reserves are of crucial importance for fighting a war. In this area, Pakistan's vulnerability was exposed. As Nawaz Sharif was to make a candid confession after the Kargil conflict that Pakistan's POL reserves could not have lasted more than five days.

The role of the Indian Navy was spectacular in the war mobilisation effort. The Eastern and Western Fleets of the Indian Navy conducted joint exercises in the Arabian Sea during the Kargil war. It was a strategic move. Originally, the Indian Navy was to conduct these exercises in the Bay of Bengal. But when Kargil crisis erupted, the venue of these exercises was shifted to the Arabian Sea.

The Indian Navy exposed the soft underbelly of Pakistan. The warships went right upto the mouth of the Gulf. With these exercises, the Indian Navy demonstrated that it was in a position to strangulate Pakistan's Karachi port-- their lifeline-- within a short time which would block all their supplies. Pakistan depends heavily on sea route for its international trade and the Karachi port is vital for this purpose. The flexing of Naval muscle decidedly unnerved Pakistan and was in a way responsible for an early end to the Kargil conflict.

As part of the war mobilisation effort, the Indian Navy installed depth charges at its various bases, besides ports and harbours, including Cochin Harbour, Bombay Harbour and Bombay High. Installation of depth charges is a fundamental precaution for preventing enemy war ships and submarines reaching close to naval establishments. Besides, vital installations like oil rigs and nuclear establishments in the western and southern parts of the country were given protection by the IAF and Indian Navy.

The war infrastructure had been put in place.

The CCS meeting on May 25 was crucial. At this meeting, the political leadership finally gave its nod for inducting the IAF into the Kargil war theater. The next morning the IAF fighters started attacking the intruders' positions in the Kargil sector. Operation Vijay had begun.

All efforts of the IAF were directed at denying the intruders any further movement across the Line of Control (LoC) into Indian territory. The Army consolidated its positions in the Kargil sector and more troops were inducted. Artillery and other equipment were also brought into this sector to provide the Indian troops with covering fire and neutralise the intruders' guns and positions. Within days of the aerial strafing, intelligence reports indicated that almost 160 of intruders had been killed. Many bodies were left under piles of stones and even the wounded were not being attended to.

Even as the involvement of the Pakistan Army was coming to light, with its SSG commandos among the intruders, attempts were continuing to supply their positions through helicopters. Pakistan responded with moving its troops into areas along the International Boundary and the LoC. At the same time, it moved more of its trained mercenaries near the LoC to further infiltrate them into the Indian territory.

Despite the aerial strafing and virtually non-stop firing from the long-range Bofors guns, hundreds more managed to infiltrate into the Indian territory. Their logistic supply lines continued to function from across the LoC and the intruders kept getting arms, ammunition, food and medicines through the Pakistani network of "mule tracks".

On the second day of the air strikes, one of the Indian MiG-27s suffered a serious mechanical problem and the pilot, Flt Lt Nachiketa, had to eject. His flying buddy, Squadron Leader Ajay Ahuja, remained over the area to look for Nachiketa. Minutes later, Ahuja's MiG-21 was shot down with a surface to air Stinger missile. Pakistan later claimed that it had captured Nachiketa while Ahuja had died. When Ahuja's body was returned to India, it was clear that he had been murdered in cold blood by his captors.

The next day, the IAF lost a Mi-17 helicopter after it had mounted an attack on Tololing in the Dras sub-sector. The chopper, too, was brought down by a Stinger missile, killing all four crew members. These were to be the last losses suffered by the IAF in an unprecedented high altitude war.

Initially, the air power was virtually wasted on inappropriate targets and the ammunition dumps and supply lines of the intruders were not hit. But that was understandable.

It was the first time in the history of IAF that its fighter bombers were required to fight high altitude warfare with Pakistani soldiers comfortably entrenched on strategic heights and armed with Stinger missiles and anti-aircraft guns.

Intruders' anti-aircraft guns did not prove to be effective at all during the Kargil war. The complete profile of an aircraft was before the intruders' anti-aircraft gunners for a very short time, which left very little reaction time for the gunners. Besides, anti-aircraft guns' rate of fire is not that effective unless guns are located all over like on an airfield. This obviously was not the case with the intruders and they had only a few anti-aircraft guns. That is why not a single IAF aircraft was hit by anti-aircraft guns Jespite the fact that the distance between the intruders' encampments and the aircraft used to be very small. What the IAF dreaded were the Stinger surface-to-air missiles. These shoulder-fired, heat-seeking missiles are manufactured by the United States and claimed to be the most lethal of this category of missiles presently available.

The CIA had given 400 of these missiles to the ISI for issue to the Afghan Mujahideen. The ISI strategists were clever. They onpassed only about half of the Stingers to the Mujahideen and retained the rest. Osama bin Laden and his band of Mujahideen put it to lethal use against the Soviets so effectively that the Stingers acquired an image of invincibility.

The IAF broke this myth during the Kargil war. After the initial losses of two aircraft, the IAF started relying on the French-built Mirage-2000 and some selected MiG-series of aircraft for strike missions. Mirage-2000 is one of the most advanced fighter aircraft in the world and has a formidable array of electronic counter measures. Before the Mirages, or for that matter even the MiGs, took off, the enemy radars used to be jammed. Mirage-2000 itself is equipped with jamming devices.

To fool the Stingers, the Mirages dropped a flare. Every object emits heat and a larger object, like an aircraft, emits larger amount of heat. Since Stingers are heat-seeking, these missiles chase the source of heat and even change their direction with the change of direction by the aircraft. Since the flares generate more heat, the Stingers lost track of the aircraft and got after the flares, while the Mirage went ahead with its assigned mission. Apart from Mirage-2000, there is only one MiG fighter which can fire flares — the MiG-27. The MiG-21s and the MiG-23s are good for ground attacks and interception. The MiG-25 is a specialist plane for high-altitude reconnaissance, while the MiG-29s are very good for air defence purposes.

The use of flares proved to be extremely effective. Not only for evading the Stinger missiles, but also for wasting the enemy Stingers. The IAF counted that the intruders fired and wasted at least 70 Stingers. Since each Stinger costs about five million rupees, the IAF could derive solace from the fact that it wasted the enemy's Stingers worth about Rs 35 crore.

The IAF's task was challenging and unenviable. It was a matter of chance that the only high altitude range, called Toshi Maidan Range, about 25 kms from Gulmarg in Kashmir valley, was available for the IAF fighters to practice high-altitude bombing. The practice sessions at the TM Range proved to be very useful in the long run.

During Operation Vijay, the IAF operations were invariably compared with NATO's air operations in Yugoslavia. But the comparison was unfair. NATO fighter aircraft were much more superior technically. Their attacks were on pre-identified fixed targets on the basis of target information furnished by the intelligence agencies. Details like location, altitude and size of the targets were fed into the computers of the NATO aircraft before the take-off. The pilot would fly over a target at an altitude of more than 25,000 feet, release the precision bomb and fly back to the base.

Most of the time these precision bombings were accurate, but occasionally there were blunders like the attack on the Chinese Embassy in Belgrade and the bombing of agricultural tractors carrying Kosovan refugees. While the Chinese Embassy was mistaken for a military target due to wrong intelligence, the convoy of tractors looked like armoured personnel carriers from the height. India could not afford precision-guided bombs because of the prohibitive costs. Each precision-guided bomb costs anywhere between Rs three crore to Rs five crore. The IAF thus made certain modifications to bring down the costs of precision-guided bombs. Air Marshal Vinod Patney, AOC-in-C of Western Air Command, has gone on record saying that the IAF did not use any laser guided bombs during the Kargil conflict because of the huge costs of these weapons.

The NATO pilots were under instruction not to descend below 15,000 feet. In contrast, the IAF pilots conducted some of the most hazardous missions in the history of air operations in the world since the Second World War. The IAF pilots took off from their base, flew to the Kargil area at an altitude of more than 25,000 feet, descended to around 20,000 feet, bombed the intruders' targets located at an altitude ranging from 13,000 feet to 17,000 feet and got away. This meant that the intruders' missiles and anti-aircraft guns' shells had to cover a distance of just about 5,000 feet to hit the IAF aircraft.

It goes to the credit of the IAF that after the initial losses, it did not suffer any more setbacks.

NATO pilots had another tremendous advantage over the Indian pilots. They had virtual fool-proof rescue mission programmes. The NATO rescue missions were as follows. When a NATO aircraft is disabled by enemy fire, the pilot ejects and simultaneously a signal emitter attached to his body is activated. The signals get picked up at the base of the rescue mission aircraft and the base orders awaiting helicopter to take off. The helicopter is escorted by fighters. The moment the helicopter takes off, its instruments lock on to the signals from the downed pilot's emitter and the helicopter reaches the pilot and picks him up.

The efficacy of the NATO rescue mission programme was tested twice. On both the occasions, the NATO rescuers reached the spot before the Yugoslav pilots. The NATO strategists took care that the signals emitted by the special device on the person of the ejected pilot emitted signals at frequently-changing frequencies which were not identifiable easily.

This is an area where the IAF will have to work in future.

The same night, the Indian troops recovered the first clinching evidence of the Pakistan Army's presence in the area of intrusions. An identity card of Sepoy Abdul Ayub, 4 Northern Light Infantry, his rucksack and personal weapon were recovered from one of the positions cleared in the Kargil sector. There were also intelligence reports of as many as 125 bodies of Pakistani soldiers being brought to Skardu and Rawalpindi.

More damning evidences of Pakistani Army's direct involvement in Kargil were to follow. A personal diary of Major Saiyed Anwar Abbasi, Company Commander, 5, Northern Light

Infantry, Pakistan Army, recovered from his dead body in Batalik, was just one of the plethora of evidence against Pakistan.

The recovered diary pad, an officially distributed notepad to any Pakistan Army company commander, had tell-tale notings, scribbled by the Company Commander himself. The notings give a graphic description of how the officer and his troops from the Northern Areas were sent to Kargil on a fruitless mission in which his entire battalion was virtually decimated—a mission which ultimately led to the sacking of the Commanding Officer, Lt Col Mohammed Tariq.

Scribbled in now-fading pencil, the first six pages of this notepad are detailed notes of a briefing given to Major Abbassi. A similar briefing must have been given to other officers as well. The notings talk about the objectives, equipment, maps and the positions which the Pakistani soldiers were to occupy. Then there are a few pages of notings made with a blue ball-point pen.

These notings show that the orders given to Major Abbassi as the task for his company were to occupy a frontage of 29 kms. This comprised of posts at heights ranging from 13,000 ft to 17,000 ft. The posted strength of his company was 2 officers, 3 Junior Commissioned Officers, 25 Non Commissioned Officers and 83 Other Ranks. However, for the execution of the intrusion task across the LoC allotted to him, Maj Abbassi had under his command only one JCO, 13 NCOs and 56 ORs.

An important fact that emerged from this diary was that during the period before the Indian Army evicted the intruders, 25 soldiers asked for evacuation owing to sickness and a number of them even asked for discharge from military service. Maj Abbasi has dropped enough indications during his journey from Skardu to Kargil as to what could be expected from this enormous misadventure of Pakistan Army. He has recorded in great details the humiliations suffered along the route. There was a serious shortage of accommodation. Sleeping bags were in short supplies. A Pakistani Army unit on the way was distinctly "discourteous" as he was only served water by them, the Major recalled.

The task allotted to the fifth battalion of NLI was to deploy in the Batalik area as per the following distribution :

* One Company at Kalubar (renamed Naeem by Pakistan Army).
* One Company at Point 5068 and Point 4100 (renamed Shaheen).
* One Company at Tharu and Kukarthang (renamed Khyber).
* One Company at Jubar (renamed Javed).
* Most significantly of all, the Commanding Officer, Lt Col Mohammad Tariq remained at Hamzigund in Pakistan's side of LoC in Northern Areas and did not even visit his troops in Kargil.

The eight Prisoners of War captured by the Indian Army, who were repatriated to Pakistan on August 27 through the International Committee of Red Cross (ICRC), were from the fifth battalion of NLI and had corroborated the notings of Maj Abbasi.

The killed Pakistani Major's diary made several significant revelations :

* The lower number of troops, than the posted strength, that came as part of the intruding company clearly demonstrated poor leadership and motivation of Pakistan Army. Being residents of the Northern Areas, it is more than likely that NLI personnel were aware of the ramifications of this misadventure.
* The high number of the Pakistani soldiers belonging to Maj Abbasi's unit who had to be evacuated -- 25 ORs-- is an important pointer to the state of their morale. Besides, there were those who asked for discharge from military service. Asking for discharge during the course of a military operation is a sure sign of low morale and dejection.
* The shortage of troops was made up by personnel from the Chitral Scouts and Bajour Scouts.

* And there is never, not even one, mention of any militant, freedom fighter or Mujahideen presence in the area of intrusion.

As the evidence of direct involvement of Pakistan Army piled up and logistic supplies to the Kargil intruders continued unabashedly from across the border, the Indian political leadership started seriously debating the most difficult and important point : whether the Indian forces should cross the LoC and smash the militant training camps and supply lines.

This was the most sensitive phase of the Kargil war. The BJP-led coalition government was divided into two camps. While on the one hand, Advani and Fernandes were vociferously advocating the need to cross the LoC (Gen Malik was game), Jaswant Singh and Brajesh Mishra were stoutly against precipitating the situation further. Singh and Mishra were in favour of resolving the crisis through other methods.

At this time, the back-channel diplomacy started in full swing. Vajpayee, willy-nilly, opted for the non-military solution.

R K Mishra, the Chief Editor of the Observer of Business and Politics, a newspaper owned by top industrialist Dhirubhai Ambani, went to Islamabad along with Vivek Katzu, a joint secretary in the MEA, in the first week of June. The two important members of the Indian back-channel diplomacy efforts, held discussions with Nawaz Sharif. Indian High Commissioner in Islamabad, G Parthasarthy, had arranged the meeting.

Their visit was followed by an equally covert trip of Niaz Naik, Pakistan former Foreign Secretary and a confidante of Nawaz Sharif. He brought a personal letter for Vajpayee from Sharif.

Naik's visit was leaked from Pakistan even as he boarded the flight to New Delhi, clearly showing that the hawks in Pakistan were itching for a military show-down and wanted to torpedo all diplomatic efforts.

Much to the embarrassment of Advani and Fernandes, Vajpayee started exclusive meetings with the Ministry of External Affairs officials every evening in June. Advani and Fernandes were kept out of these meetings. These meetings, which continued for about ten days, generated a lot of heat within the government as Advani and Fernandes did not approve of these.

Advani had been stressing the need for taking a strong deterrent action against Pakistan, and quickly, because he feared that any delays were likely to bring in international pressures on India. What Advani had been asking for was not necessarily crossing the LoC, but giving a befitting reply to Pakistan, especially in the wake of the arrival of mutilated bodies of six Indian soldiers, who were taken captive by Pakistan and were tortured to death.

Advani said at the behind-the-door parleys that options other than crossing the LoC should be explored. Hitting the militant training camps and the supply lines in the POK with surface-to-surface missiles was one such option. But that option also was ruled out in view of the escalatory nature of such strikes.

The Vajpayee government, at this stage, also discussed with several countries, including Russia, whether they could give such guns which had an effective firing range of more than 75 kilometres. The Bofors guns, available with the Indian Army, were highly effective, but their shells could land only upto 30-35 kms. This option, too, had to be given up as not a single country possessed guns which had a range of more than 75 kms.

In the meanwhile, the inevitable happened. US President Bill Clinton rang up Vajpayee for the first time on June 14.

Clinton told Vajpayee that he was aware that the Pakistani troops, and not Mujahideen as claimed by Islamabad, had intruded into the Indian territory and that he was pressuring Nawaz Sharif to pull out his troops from Kargil. Clinton asked Vajpayee to keep exercising the restraint the Indian government had shown thus far and not precipitate the matters further.

This was a subtle diplomatic victory for Pakistan. India had been maintaining, and continued to maintain throughout the entire Kargil conflict, that it would not agree to a third party mediation on the question of Kashmir.

As a demonstration of this stand, Vajpayee had declined the offer of Clinton for talks in Washington as the days indicated by Clinton to Vajpayee for the latter's Washington visit coincided with Nawaz Sharif's visit to the US. Vajpayee thanked Clinton for the offer but made it clear that his visit to Washington at that time would tantamount to a third party mediation.

But, as the events were to unfold, the US eventually emerged as a mediating third party, though Washington and New Delhi steadfastly denied it.

Vajpayee soon realised that his exclusive meetings with the MEA officials had the potential of causing a serious rift between him and Advani. Initially, he took Advani into confidence and later on discontinued with these meetings with the MEA officials. But he continued with the back-channel diplomacy.

Leaders of the Rashtriya Swayamsewak Sangh (RSS), a powerful cadre-based organisation which serves as the BJP's base across India, were very sore with Vajpayee over his alleged dithering on the question of crossing the LoC. They were of the view that the Kargil crisis was a god-sent opportunity to deal with the problem of Pakistan-backed terrorism at one stroke by smashing all terrorist training camps in Pakistan.

The RSS leaders told Vajpayee without mincing words that he was committing the same mistake which the then Prime Minister, Jawahar Lal Nehru, had committed during the 1962 war with China. But Vajpayee ignored these harsh comments. On one occasion, Jaswant Singh, snubbed the RSS when he said tackling the Kargil crisis was the government's affair and not that of the RSS.

At one of the meetings of the CCS, Vajpayee went at great lengths to elaborate why he was favouring back-channel diplomacy to an outright military solution to the problem. He warned that the situation was explosive as both India and Pakistan were nuclear powers and irresponsible Generals of Pakistan Army were capable of pushing the sub-continent into a nuclear war in which there will be no winners.

An important question that arose during the Kargil conflict was the so-called intelligence failure.

Strange though it may seem, there were intelligence reports of large presence of "Mujahideen-like" people in the POK across the LoC as early as August-September 1998. In fact, the BSF had submitted two reports to the Army authorities-- one on November 28, 1998 and another on December 12, 1998-- warning of infiltration of intruders in the Kargil Sector.

The BSF, for some strange reasons, had been asked by the Indian Army to stay put at the strategic Chorbatla posts during the 1998-1999 winter season when the Army had vacated its own posts. Nobody knows why the Army did this. The Army obviously had much superior firepower and better trained personnel than the BSF.

It was the BSF personnel perched atop Chorbatla, located between Batalik and Turtuk, who noticed the first infiltration in November end. The BSF intelligence reports, thus, knock the bottom out of the claims of the Indian Ministry of Defence that the Pakistani intruders occupied the Kargil heights in April only.

Brigadier Surendra Singh, who was later transferred out of the Kargil sector during the crisis, had claimed that he had sent several reports warning of the Pakistani infiltration. But this, too, is far from the truth.

In that limited sense, the intelligence agencies had failed. Limited because whatever intelligence reports were available were enough to jolt the Indian Army out of its complacence and take prompt counter measures.

But there was not a single intelligence report, either from the Indian Army or any other Indian agency, which specifically talked about the massive incursion by Pakistan Army regulars into the Indian territory. All these reports merely talked of "infiltration" by suspected militants. None revealed the actual Pakistani gameplan.

It was strange indeed that whatever reports various intelligence and other agencies had filed about Kargil, the Corps Commander, the Division Commander and the Army Commander did not take concrete measures to thwart the Pakistani gameplan and allowed the Pakistanis to surprise India.

Quite inexplicably, Gen Malik went ahead with his Poland visit when the Kargil crisis erupted. He remained in Poland for ten days even after the Indian Army had discovered the Pakistani intrusion and came back after completing his visit only on May 19, 1999. This when he was kept informed on a day-to-day basis about the Indian Army operations in Kargil through the coded military channels. Interstingly, the Army Commander, Lt Gen H M Khanna too proceeded to his home town for a few days even after the Kargil crisis had surfaced.

The 15 Corps, with its headquarters in Srinagar, has one of the largest fleets of reconnaissance aircraft and helicopters. These aircraft did make dozens of sorties also during the December-April period. But still it was left to some local people who reported to the civic authorities of movement of foreigner-looking people in the mountains.

The massive fortification done by the Pakistanis and their free movements -- the Pakistani soldiers were routinely going for hunting and were opening fire from their guns to kill boredom--should not have escaped the notice of the Indian reconnaissance missions.

But it did. The reasons of this need to be shared with the Indian citizens and exemplary punishment needs to be given to those found guilty of dereliction of duty.

Then only more Kargils can be averted.

2 A Man Called Pervez Musharraf

There was nothing striking about one particular Pakistani Brigadier when he had caught the eye of President Zia ul-Haq in the 1980s. The Brigadier perhaps had one characteristic which struck a chord in Gen Zia's heart. Like the Chief Martial Law Administrator, the Brigadier was a devout Deobandi and was in the good books of the Jamaat-e-Islami.

The Brigadier had the knack of winning friends and influencing people at the right places at the right time. He did so with Gen Zia also.The Pakistani President entrusted the Brigadier a crucial task of training the Afghan Mujahideen who were then engaged in intense fighting with the Soviet occupationist forces.

The Brigadier made full use of this opportunity to catapult his career. During this period he made friends with another influential man who was to hold the Islamic world in sway a few years later : Osama bin Laden. The CIA watched the Brigadier's performance in Afghanistan with mixed feelings. While it was all praise for his anti-Soviet work, it watched with concern as his newly-made links with narcotic barons of the North West Frontier Province (NWFP) went from strength to strength.

In 1987, Gen Zia gave another important assignment to the Brigadier who had proven his worth by then. The SSG had just then raised a base at Khapalu in Siachen area and he was asked to command it. In a bid to raise his stock further with Gen Zia, he embarked on a misadventure. He organised his SSG commandos to launch an attack on an Indian post in Bilafond La in September that year, only to be beaten back.

The Bilafond La misadventure was to pale into insignificance eleven years later. It had to be. The enormity of misadventure had to increase in direct proportion to his rise to the highest office a soldier can aspire to.

The Brigadier had become Chief of Army Staff on October 8, 1998. General Pervez Musharraf was thus catapulted into the hottest and the most crucial seat of power in Pakistan.

Within days of his assuming office, the Pakistan Army had started work on Pakistan's biggest misadventure yet : the Kargil infiltration. Gen Musharraf was one man who played a pivotal role in planning and executing the Kargil infiltration. He took into confidence only a handful of Generals and even Nawaz Sharif was informed at an advanced stage of the operation.

Gen Musharraf is said to have kicked the very ladder he used for climbing up in his career : Prime Minister Nawaz Sharif. Though a blue-eyed boy of Sharif, Musharraf's good relations with Sharif could not last even six months after he was made the Chief of Army Staff.

Gen Musharraf, like Lt Gen Ziauddin who was made ISI Chief by Sharif, was hand-picked by the Pakistani Premier. He superseded Lt Gen Ali Kuli Khan and Lt Gen Khalid Nawaz, both of whom quit after Musharraf's surprise appointment. Gen Kuli Khan, a Pakhtoon who held the post of Chief of General Staff, was a critic of Nawaz Sharif. So was Gen Nawaz, a Punjabi who was the Quarter Master General. In fact, when Gen Jehangir Karamat was the Pakistan Army Chief, Gen Nawaz had openly criticised the functioning of the Nawaz Sharif government at several conferences of the Corps Commanders.

The choice of Musharraf as COAS was strange because he is a Mohajir of Azamgarh/Karachi origin, though it is another matter that he detests Mohajirs. He settled down in Gujranawala in Punjab and preferes to project himself as a Punjabi rather than a Mohajir. His hatred towards the Muttahida Qaumi Movement (MQM) and its Chief, Altaf Hussain, is well-known.

In September 1995, when Benazir Bhutto was the Prime Minister, the Pakistani Customs had seized a car in the NWFP on charges of illegally carrying huge quantities of arms and ammunition. (This incident has been given in details elsewhere in this book.) Investigations into the incident led to a stunning disclosure that the arms cache was meant for some disgruntled elements in Pakistan Army, who wanted to overthrow the Benazir Bhutto government and install Gen Musharraf as head of the Islamic State.

Gen Mohd Aziz was also said to be involved in the plot. Gen Aziz is the same Pakistan Army officer who figures prominently in the intercepted conversation he had with Gen Musharraf twice in May 1999. (Transcripts of the two intercepted conversations have been reproduced later in this chapter.) However, no action could be taken against Musharraf or Aziz for want of evidence.

All this, coupled with a strong recommendation from the Jamaat-e-Islami, was an important reason in Musharraf's appointment as Army Chief. There was another reason also, which unravels the Machiavellian aspect of his personality. He constantly kept Nawaz Sharif informed of the acts and utterances of Gen Kuli Khan and Gen Nawaz. Over and above all this, he was vociferously backed by none other than President Mohd Rafique Tarar, a former Judge, and Lt Gen (retd) Javed Nasir, formerly head of ISI. Both Tarar and Nasir are considered to be very close to Sharif.

The relations between Sharif and Musharraf did not remain smooth for long. By March 1999, a noticeable degree of coldness had crept into their relationship.

Musharraf realised that by making him the COAS, Sharif had sought to kill two birds with one stone : tackling the Mohajir movement and the MQM factor by making a Mohajir the Army Chief even at the risk of discontentment in the ranks of the Punjabi-dominated army; and secondly, to terrorise and finish his political opponent, Benazir Bhutto. Immediately after his appointment as army chief, Musharraf did the bidding of Sharif by setting up special military courts in Karachi to conduct summary trials of the arrested MQM cadres. These courts quickly pronounced death sentence on several MQM cadres. Two of them were even executed before the Pakistani Supreme Court declared these courts unconstitutional.

Pakistani press was full of criticism of such courts. Sharif's plan was reported to be sinister. Through these courts, it was alleged, Sharif wanted to settle political scores with Benazir Bhutto and execute her jailed husband, Asif Ali Zardari, as a "terrorist" in connection with the killing of Benazir's brother, Murtaza.

When the Sharif-Musharraf equation was good, the Prime Minister made his army chief in charge of the Water and Power Development Authority (WAPDA). Musharraf was given a three-point charter of duties as far as WAPDA was concerned : root out corruption, tackle labour unrest, and tone up its efficiency.

But from March 1999 onwards, Musharraf started expanding his power base in WAPDA. Much to the chagrin of Sharif, he passed an order that in capacity of the supervisory authority, the army would henceforth conduct all negotiations with the independent power producers.

This order clearly meant clipping the wings of the politicians and bureaucrats. Sharif asked Musharraf to rescind this order, but he declined to oblige.

As if this were not enough, Musharraf ordered for preparation of a list of all those who had not paid their bills to the WAPDA. The WAPDA defaulters' list was prepared on a war footing and gave a stick to Musharraf to beat Sharif with.

The Sharif government was in for a major embarrassment when the name of a Shia woman in his Cabinet, Abida Hussain, had been leaked to the press as a major defaulter of WAPDA's dues. Abida had to quit the government.

It was an open secret that Musharraf was behind this leakage, though, of course, he has never admitted it. To add insult to injury, stories appeared in the Pakistani media that Sharif's family itself topped the list of defaulters. Nobody disputed the source of these reports this time also.

Gen Musharraf views ISI Chief Lt Gen Ziauddin as his rival. Like many senior Generals, Gen Ziauddin, too, was aware of Musharraf's plans to infiltrate Pakistani regulars into Kargil. The Kargil plan was discussed in details by the Pakistani top brass. Gen Nasir, who for some cynical reasons holds a very poor opinion of the Indian Army, supported Musharraf in the latter's quest for annexing Kashmir by stepping up covert action.

The sole voice of dissent came from the ISI Chief. Gen Ziauddin argued that the plan was bound to trigger off a strong military reprisal from India which could snowball into a full-scale war. Ziauddin also warned that this assertion of Islamic fundamentalism could alienate Washington from Islamabad.

But Musharraf ignored Ziauddin's warning on the likely problems Pakistan could face with the US and went ahead with the plan. In early February 1999, Musharraf decided to shift bin Laden's Mujahideen brigade from Jalalabad (Afghanistan) to Kargil where some of his army jawans were already camping, taking full advantage of the fact that the Indian Army used to traditionally vacate its posts in the Kargil sector during winters.

Sharif cleared this plan, too. Ironically, Sharif's approval came a few days after US Deputy Secretary of State, Strobe Talbott, had visited Pakistan.

Bin Laden's Mujahideen were infiltrating into Kargil even as Islamabad was talking peace with New Delhi and the Lahore Declaration was being adopted. From then on, Musharraf had not kept Sharif informed on a day-to-day basis of the Kargil situation, which was to explode a few months later.

Musharraf is a staunch Sunni Muslim and is sectarian to the core. His hatred for Shia Muslims is well known. He demonstrated it in May 1988 in Gilgit when this Shia-dominated region raised a banner of revolt. The Shias of Gilgit had many grievances. They were being controlled by nominees from Islamabad, who were Sunnis and were viewed as outsiders.

Gen Zia entrusted Musharraf, who had by now become his confidante, with the task of quelling this rebellion in Gilgit. He unleashed an unparralleled wave of terror and cruelty to teach the local Shias a lesson. He brought thousands of tribesmen, armed to the teeth, from outside Gilgit. The marauders burnt houses and standing crops, raped women and murdered people. This reign of terror continued for days. Nobody stopped them. Hundreds of Shias were killed during this Rape of Gilgit.

Musharraf's hatred against Shias is a key to his personality and explains why he embarked on the Kargil plan immediately after he became army chief. Like Gilgit, Kargil, too, is a Shia-dominated region. And the master stroke of his strategy was that he chose soldiers from the Northern Areas, a Shia-dominated region, to infiltrate into Kargil.

Immediately after becoming the Army Chief, Gen Musharraf had brought his protege, Lt Gen Aziz, who was then the ISI Chief, to the Army Headquarters. Aziz was given the key post of Chief of General Staff and was made personally responsible for implementation of the Kargil operation. Musharraf had directed his Military Intelligence chief to work in close coordination with Aziz.

The Musharraf-Aziz special relationship is clearly reflected in the intercepted conversations between the two. The intercepts, being reproduced below, also indicate the cooling of relations between Sharif and Musharraf :

Verbatim record of full conversation of May 26, 1999 original conversation in Urdu and English. Portions translated into English are in italics.

Pak end - Lt. Gen. Mohd. Aziz, Chief of General Staff

China end - Gen. Pervez Musharraf, Chief of Army Staff

China end(C) - I am sorry the line is busy now.

Pak end (P) - Can I hold ? Salam-ale-qum Sir.

C - Wale-Qum-Salam.

P - Sir, *there is a call from Pakistan.* Gen Pervez Musharraf.

C - *Yes Sir.*

P - *Gen Aziz Khan will speak.*

C - *Yes.*

P - Sir, Col Hassan.

C - Yes Hassan.

P - *Sir, how are you?*

C - *Grace of God*

P - *Sir, please speak, Hello.*

C - Thank you.

P - Sir, Salam-ale-qum.

C - *Yes Aziz, how are you ?*

P - Very fine, Sir. How is the visit going?

C - *Yes, very well. OK. And, what else is the news on that side?*

P - Ham-dul-ullah. There is no change on the ground situation. *They have started* rocketing and straffing. *That has been upgraded a little.* It had happened yesterday also and today. *Today* high altitude bombing *has been done.*

C - *On their side, in those positions* ?

P - *In those positions, but in today's bombing about* 3 bombs landed in our side of Line of Control. No damage, Sir.

C - *Is it quite a lot ?*

P - Sir, about 12-13 bombs *were dropped,* from which 3 fell on our side, which does not appear to be a result of inaccuracy. *In my* interpretation, it is a sort of giving of a message *that if need be we can do it on the other side as well.* It is quite distance apart. *Where the bombs have been dropped, they have tried to drop from a good position where they are in difficulty, from behind the LOC* but they have fallen on our side of the LOC. *So I have spoken to the* Foreign Secretary *and I have told him that he should make the appropriate noises about this in the Press.*

C - *They (Indians) should also be told.*

P - *That we have told,* Foreign Secretary *will also say and* Rashid *will also say. He will not, generally speaking, make any such mistake about those other bombs falling on the other side, our stand should be that all these bombs are falling on our side. We will not come into that situation.* The guideline *that they have given, we have stressed that we should say that this* build-up and employment of air strike *which has been done under the* garb of ..... us (?), actually they are targetting our position on the LOC and our logistic build-up, these possibly they are taking under the garb having intention for operation the craft (?) Line of Control, and this need to be taken note of and we would retaliate in kind ..... is what happened? *So, the entire build up we want to give this colour.*

C - *Absolutely* OK. Yes, this is better. *After that, has there been any talk with them? Any meetings etc. ?*

P - *Yesterday, again, in the evening.*

C - *Who all were there ?*

P - Actually, we insisted *that a meeting should be held, because otherwise that friend of ours, the incumbent of my old chair, we thought lest he give some interpretation of his own, we should do something ourselves by going there.*

C - *Was he little disturbed. I heard that there was some trouble in* Sialkot.

P - *Yes. There was one in Daska. On this issue there was trouble. Yes, he was little disturbed about that but I told him that such small things keep happening....(?) and we can reply to such things in a better way.*

C - *Absolutely.*

P - *There is no such thing to worry.*

C - *So that briefing to Mian Saheb that we did, was the forum the same as where we had done previously ? There, at Jamshed's place ?*

P - *No. In Mian Saheb's office.*

C - *Oh I see. There. What was he saying ?*

P - *From here we had gone* - Choudhary Zafar Saheb, Mehmood, myself & Tauqir.* *Because before going, Tauqir had spoken with his conterpart. We carried that tape with us.*

C - *So, what was he (Indian counterpart) saying ?*

P - *That is very interesting. When you come, I will play it for you. Its focus was that these infiltrators who are sitting here, they have your help and* artillery support, *without which they could not have come to J & K.* This is not a very friendly act and it is against the spirit of the Lahore Declaration. *Then Tauqir told him that if your boys tried to physically attack the* Line of Control and go beyond it .... and that the bombs were planted on the Turtok bridge and the dead body received in the process was returned with military honours and I said, I thought that there was good enough indication *you would not enter into this*

---

* This is a reference to Maj Gen Tauqir Zia, the Pakistani Director General of Military Operations (DGMO). The next line refers to a conversation he had with the Indian DGMO, Lt Gen N C ViJ.

type of misadventure, and all this build up that you are doing - one or more brigade strength and 50-60 aircraft *are being collected,* these are excuses for undertaking some operations against the various spaces, *so I had put him on the* defensive. *Then he said the same old story. He would put three points again and again that they (militants) should not be supported,* and without your support they could not be there, *they have* sophisticated weapons and *we will* flush them out, we will not let them stay there. But this is not a friendly act.

C - *So, did they talk of coming out and meeting somewhere ?*

P - *No, No, they did not.*

C - *Was there some other talk of putting pressure on us ?*

P - *No.* He only said that they (militants) will be given suitable reception, *this Term he used. He said, they will be flushed out, and everytime Tauqir said that please tell us some detail, detail about how many have gone into your area,* what *is happening there?* Then I will ask the concerned people and then we will get back to you. *So whenever he asked these details,* he would say, we will talk about this when we meet, then I will give details. This means, they are possibly looking forward to next round of talks, in which the two sides could meet. *This could be the next round of talks between the* two PMs which they are expecting it...... Sir, very good thing, no problem......

C - *So, many times we had discussed, taken your* (PM's?..) blessings and *yesterday also I told him* that the door of discussion, dialogue must be kept open and rest, no change in ground situation.

P - *So, no one was in a particularly disturbed frame of mind.*

C - *Even your seat man ?*

P - *Yes, he was disturbed. Also, Malik Saheb was disturbed, as they had been even earlier. Those two's views were that the* status quo and the present position of Gen Hassan *(?) no change should be* recommended *in that. But he was also saying that any escalation after that should be* regulated *as there may be the danger* of war. *On this* logic, *we gave the* suggestion *that there was no such fear as the scruff (tooti) of* their (militants) *neck is in our hands, whenever you want, we could* regulate *it. Ch Zafar Saheb coped very well. He gave a very good presentation of* our viewpoint. *He said we had briefed the PM earlier and given an* assessment. *After this, we played the tape of Tauqir. Then he said that what we are seeing, that was our assessment, and those very stages of the military situation were being seen, which it would not be a problem for us to handle. Rest, it was for your guidance how to deal with the political and diplomatic aspects. We told him there is no reason of alarm and panic. Then he said that when I came to know 7 days back, when Corps Commanders were told. The entire reason for the success of this operation was this total secrecy. Our experience was that our earlier efforts failed because of lack of secrecy. So, the top priority is to accord confidentiality, to ensure our success. We should respect this and the advantage we have from this would give us a handle.*

C - *Rest (baki), is Mian Saheb OK?*

P - *OK. He was confident just like that but for the other two. Shamshad as usual was supporting. Today, for the last two hours the BBC has been continuously reporting on the air strikes by India. Keep using this - let them keep dropping bombs. As far as internationalisation is concerned, this is the fastest this has happened. You may have seen in the Press about UN Secretary General Kofi Annan's appeal that both countries should sit and talk.*

C - *This is very good.*

P - Yes, this is very good.

C - OK, Bye.

Verbatim record of full conversation of May 29, 1999 original conversation in Urdu and English. Portions translated into English are in italics

Pak end - Lt Gen Mohd Aziz, Chief of General Staff

China end - Gen Pervez Musharraf, Chief of Army Staff

Pak end (P) - This is Pakistan. Give me room no. 83315 (same room number). Hello.

China end (C) - Hello Aziz.

P. - The situation on ground is OK, no change. This area but it is not brought down by attack. One of their MI-17 arms (?) was brought down. *Further, the position is,* we had approached to our position, it *was brought down.* Rest is OK. Nothing else except, there is a development. Have you listened to yesterday's news regarding Mian Saheb speaking to his counterpart. He told him that the spirit of Lahore Declaration and escalation has been done by your people. Specially wanted to speak to me thereafter. He told Indian PM that they should have waited instead of upping the ante by using Air Force and all other means. He (Nawaz) told him (Indian PM) that he suggested Sartaj Aziz could go to New Delhi to explore the possibility of defusing the tension.

C - OK.

- Which is likely to take place, most probably tomorrow.
- OK.
- Our other friend (Lt Gen Ziauddin, DG ISI...?... or could be United States) might have also put pressure on. For that, today they will have a discussion at Foreign Office about 9.30 and Zafar Saheb (Lt Gen Saeeduz Zaman Zafar, GOC 11 Corps and Acting Chief) is supposed to attend.
- OK.
- Aziz Saheb (Sartaj Aziz, Foreign Minister) has discussed with me and my recommendation is that dialogue option is always open.. But in their first meeting, they must give no understanding or no commitment on ground situation.
- Very correct. You or Mehmood (GOC X Corps, Rawalpindi) must have to go with Zafar. Because, they don't know about the ground situation.
- This week, we are getting together at 8'O clock because meeting will be at 9.30, so Zafar Saheb will deliberate it. We want to suggest to Zafar that they have to maintain that they will not be talking about ground situation. All that you say. So far as the ground situation is concerned. Subsequently, DGMOs can discuss with each other and work out the modus operandi.
- Idea on LoC.
- Yes, Hint is that, given that the LoC has many areas where the interpretation of either side is not what the other side believes. So, comprehensive deliberation is required. So, that can be worked out by DGMOs.
- If they are assured that we are here from a long period. We have been sitting here for long. Like in the beginning, the matter is the same - no post was attacked and no post was captured. The situation is that we are along our defensive Line of Control. If it is not in his (Sartaj Aziz's) knowledge, then discuss it altogether. Emphasise that for years, we are here only.

C - Yes, this point should be raised. We are sitting on th same LoC since a long period.

P - This is their weakness. They are not agreed on th demarcation under UN's verification, whereas we ar agreed. We want to exploit it.

C - This is in Simla Agreement that we cannot go for U intervention.

P - Our neighbour does not accept their presence c UNMOGIP arrangement for survey for the area. So, w can start from the top, from 9842 (NJ 9842). On thi line, we can give them logic but in short, th recommendation for Sartaj Aziz Saheb is that he shoul make no commitment in the first meeting on militar situation. And he should not even accept ceasefir because if there is ceasefire, then vehicles will be movin (on Dras-Kargil highway). In this regard, they have t use their own argument that whatever is interfering wit you. That we don't know but there is no justificatio about tension on LoC. No justification. We want to giv them this type of brief so that he does not get into an specifics.

C - Alright.

P - In this connection, we want your approval and what i your programme.

C - I will come tomorrow. We are just leaving within a hour. We are going to Shenzhen. From there, by evening we will be in Hong Kong. There will be a flight tomorro from Hong Kong. So, we will be there at Lahore in th evening, via Bangkok flight.

P - Sunday evening, you will be at Lahore. We will als indicate that, if there is more critical situation, then (Sartaj visit) should be deferred for another day or tw We can discuss on Monday and then do.

C - Has this MI-17 not fallen in our area ?

P - No Sir. This has fallen in their area. We have not claimed it. We have got it claimed through the Mujahideen.

C - Well done.

P - But topwise side, crashing straight before our eyes.

C - Very good. *Now are they facing any greater difficulty in flying them ? Are they scared or not ? This also you should note. Are they coming any less nearer ?*

P - Yes, *There is lot of pressure on them.* They were talking about greater air defence than they had anticipated. They can't afford to lose any more aircraft. There has been less intensity of air flying after that.

C - Very good. First class. Is there any build up on the ground ?

P - Just like that but the movement is pretty sluggish and slow. *One or two are coming near no. 6.* Till now only one call sign in which one has not reached the valley so far. Now the air people and the ground people will stay back and then the situation will be OK.

C - See you in the evening.

3 OPERATION TOPAC

The Pakistani dictator, General Zia ul-Haq, died in a mysterious plane crash on August 17, 1988. But not before he had put Pakistan on road to a diabolical anti-India plan. The plan, codenamed "Operation Topac", is still under implementation. The Kargil intrusion was Phase 2 of Operation Topac.

Four months before his death, Gen Zia called a meeting of top Army Generals and ISI officials at his residential office. The meeting was a hush-hush affair. Intelligence reports indicated that a top Afghan Mujahideen leader and two prominent Kashmir terrorists also attended the secret meeting. President Zia delivered a crucial speech at this meeting. Zia unveiled Operation Topac in his speech. Operation Topac was meant to be a new version of "Operation Gibraltar" — an anti-India Pakistani operation which flopped in 1965.

In an intelligence coup of sorts for India, a few months after Zia presented Operation Topac before his top Generals, the Indian intelligence agencies were given by a friendly intelligence agency a copy of Zia's speech delivered at the April conclave. The speech was reproduced in the April-June 1999 issue of the prestigious "Indian Defence Review" (IDR) as follows :

Gentlemen, I have spoken on this subject before, therefore, I will leave out the details. As you know due to our preoccupation in Afghanistan, in the service of Islam, I have not been able to put these plans before you earlier. Let there be no mistake, however, that our aim remains quite clear and firm — the liberation of the Kashmir Valley— our Muslim Kashmiri brothers cannot be allowed to stay with India for any length of time, now.

In the past we had opted for hamhanded military options and therefore, failed. So, as I have mentioned before, we will now keep our military option for the last moment as a coup de grace, if and when necessary. Our Kashmiri brethern in the valley, though with us in their hearts and minds, are simple-minded folk and do not easily take to the type of warfare to which, say, a Punjabi or an Afghan takes to naturally, against foreign domination. The Kashmiris, however, have a few qualities which we can exploit. First, his shrewdness and intelligence; second, his power to persevere under pressure; and the third, if I may so say, he is a master of political intrigue. If we provide him means through which he can best utilise these qualities— he will deliver the goods. Sheer brute force is in any case not needed in every type of warfare, especially so in the situation obtaining in the Kashmir Valley, as I have explained earlier.

Here we must adopt these methods of combat which the Kashmiri mind can grasp and cope with — in other words, a coordinated use of moral and physical means, other than military operations, which will destroy the will of the enemy, damage his political capacity and expose him to the world as an aggressor. This aim, Gentlemen, shall be achieved in the initial phases.

In the first phase, which may, if necessary, last a couple of years. We will assist our Kashmiri brethern in getting hold of the power apparatus of the State by political subversion and intrigue. I would like to mention here that as no Government can survive in Occupied Kashmir unless it has the tacit approval of Delhi, it would be unrealistic to believe that the MUF or any such organisation can seize power through democratic or other means. In view of this, power must "apparently" remain with those whom New Delhi favours. We must therefore ensure that certain "favoured politicians" from the ruling elite be selected who would collaborate with us in subverting all effective organs of the State. In brief, our plan for Kashmir, which will be codenamed as "Op Topac" will be as follows :

PHASE 1

A low-level insurgency against the regime so that it is under seige, but does not collpase as we would not yet want central rule imposed by Delhi.

We plant our chosen men in all the key positions; they will subvert the police forces, financial institutions, the communication network and other important organisations.

We whip up anti-Indian feelings amongst the students and peasants, preferably on some religious issues, so that we can enlist their active support for rioting and anti-government demonstrations.

Organise and train subversive elements and armed groups with capabilities, initially, to deal with para-military forces located in the valley.

Adopt and develop means to cut off lines of communications between Jammu and Kashmir and within Kashmir and Ladakh by stealth, without recourse to force. The road over Zojila upto Kargil and the road over Khardungla should receive our special attention.

In collaboration with Sikh extremists, create chaos and terror in Jammu to divert attention from the valley at a critical juncture and discredit the regime even in the Hindu mind.

Establish virtual control in those parts of the Kashmir valley where the Indian Army is not located or deployed. The Southern Kashmir Valley may be one such region.

PHASE 2

Exert maximum pressure on the Siachen, Kargil and Rajauri-Punch sectors to force the Indian Army to deploy reserve formations outside the main Kashmir Valley.

Attack and destroy base depots and HQ located at Srinagar, Pattan, Kupwara, Baramulla, Bandipur and Chowkiwala by covert action at a given time.

Some Afghan Mujahideen, by then settled in Azad Kashmir, will then infiltrate in selected pockets with a view to extending areas of our influence. This aspect will require detailed and ingenious planning. The fiasco of Op Gibraltar (1965) holds many lessons for us here.

Finally a Special Force under selected retired officers belonging to Azad Kashmir, with the hard core consisting of Afghans, will be ready to attack and destroy airfields, radio stations, block Banihal Tunnel and Kárgil-Leh Highway.

At a certain stage of the operations, Punjab and adjacent areas of Jammu and Kashmir will be put under maximum pressure internally by our offensive posture.

PHASE 3

Detailed plans for the liberation of Kashmir Valley and establishment of an independent Islamic State in the third phase will follow.

We do not have much time. Maximum pressure must be exerted before the general elections in India and before Indian Army reserves, which are still bogged down in Sri Lanka, become available. By the Grace of God, we have managed to accumulate large stocks of modern arms and ammunition from US consignments intended for Afghan Mujahideen. This will help our Kashmiri brethern achieve their goals. Even if we create a kind of "Azad Kashmir" in some remote parts of Occupied Kashmir as a beginning, the next step may not be as difficult as it appears today. On the other hand, it should also be noted that a part of the Indian Army, particularly the Infantry, will be well trained by now for such a situation due to their experience in the North-eastern region and more recently in Sri Lanka. But the situation in Kashmir will be somewhat different; more like the "Intefada" of Palestinians in towns, and on the pattern of the Mujahideen in the countryside to attack hard targets. A period of chaos in the State is essential in the circumstances.

And what of our Chinese friends ? They can do no more than ensure that Indian forces deployed against them are not moved out : but this may be required only at the last or the third stage of our operations. Of course, if we are in serious trouble, the Chinese and our other powerful friends shall come to our rescue one way or the other. They will ensure if we do not win, at least we don't lose.

Finally, I wish to caution you once more that it will be disastrous to believe that we can take on India in a straight contest. We must, therefore, be careful and maintain a low military profile so that the Indians do not find an excuse to pre-empt us, by attacking at a time and at a point of their own choosing, at least before Phase 1 and 2 of the Operation are over. We must pause and assess the course of operations after each phase, as our strategy and plans may require drastic changes in certain circumstances. I need not emphasise any further than a deliberate and objective assessment of the situation must be ensured at each stage, otherwise a stalemate will follow with no good for Pakistan. Pakistan Paindabad.

Despite the timely intelligence, there was no political will from the successive governments to take Pakistan head on and try to nip the problem in the bud. The Pakistani audacity and resolve was apparent from the fact that Op Topac was prepared an year after India had flexed its military muscle in the famous Operation Brasstacks of 1987.

Gen Zia's death, the eventual political turmoil and Pakistan's continued involvement in Afghanistan were some of the factors that delayed the implementation of Op Topac. The Operation started with full steam from 1989 onwards. Around this time, Pakistan military strategists had also prepared blueprints of two more operations : Op Mushtary (Jupiter) and Plan X.

Maj Gen Afsir Karim (Retd), a much-decorated Indian soldier who is also a member of the National Security Council Advisory Board, wrote in IDR that Op Mushtary will commence at a certain stage of Zarb-e-Kamil and is likely to take the following form :

* Extensive and continued firing including artillery and mortar fire all along the Line of Control.

* Attack on isolated posts on the LoC, particularly in remote and difficult areas.

* Capture of important but less defencible tactical features on the Shamsabari Range, Kargil, Shyok Valley - Saltoro Range and in the Punch-Rajauri sector.

Plan X was prepared to pre-empt a possible Indian military offensive in Pakistan Occupied Kashmir and force an Indian retreat from the Saltoro Crest Line and Siachen Glacier. Plan X also envisaged launching a surprise attack to seize and hold logistics support bases vital for maintenance of troops deployed on the Saltoro Crest Line, Siachen and Southern Glaciers.

The Pakistani military strategists who prepared Plan X reasoned that such a surprise offensive would trap all Indian troops deployed in the Glacier areas and enable Pakistan to negotiate withdrawal of Indian forces from Siachen Glacier from a position of strength.

The IDR (April-June 1999) published as follows the main features of Plan X made available to India by an intelligence agency of a third country :

* To achieve surprise, Plan X was to be executed in deep winter, preferably at a time when flights between Thoise (a forward air base of IAF in Ladakh) and the rest of India are unable to operate when the strategic Khardungla is blocked due to heavy snowfall.

* Capture of forward positions of Partapur garrison astride Siari-Turtuk axis and logistics support bases for Southern Glaciers by infiltration across the LoC.

* Heli-dropping of specially equipped and trained troops east of Partapur-Thoise and Siachen Base Camp; with the task of capturing Thoise Airfield complex and Siachen Base simultaneously.

* Interdiction of Khardungla by SSG commandos after blowing up sections of road and important culverts on either side of the pass.

* Actual concentration of troops and simulation of major attacks at an appropriate time in Dras, Kargil, Gurez, Tangdhar and Punch sectors to tie down Indian reserve formations.

* Raids and destruction of staging camps and gun positions located on the Siachen Glacier. Exert maximum pressure on Indian posts on the crest line from both sides of the LoC, Capture Sia La on the crest line in the northern Glacier area, if possible.

* Step up guerilla and terrorist activity, raid airfields and radar facilities in the valley on given code words.

* Activate major disturbances and widespread rioting in all major towns of Kashmir Valley and Jammu Division.

* All forces to be prepared and trained to operate for a period of eight days without resupply or land link-up.

* Plans for exfiltration of troops in unfavourable circumstances will be prepared but divulged only to a selected few.

4 Making of the Line of Control

A satellite imagery of the Line of Control was taken during October 1998. It revealed that there was no military activity in the area. There was no intrusion either.

Air photographs of the area during this period also highlighted the regular posts on both sides of the LoC. This is clearly demonstrative of the fact that the ground troops of India and Pakistan were aware of the alignment of the LoC and the Pakistani objections to the LoC were merely an afterthought, a smoke-screen to cover their military intent of aligning the LoC to their advantage.

Why then the Pakistani military officials and politicians suddenly started harping on, what they called, the "undemarcated" LoC? Obviously, the Pakistanis were looking for "credible" excuses to justify the Kargil incursion.

In so doing, the Pakistani officials sought to turn a blind eye to historical facts which are incontrovertible and beyond doubt or dispute. The LoC was meticulously discussed, surveyed wherever necessary, identified on ground and delineated on maps giving detailed grid references and description of landmarks. These were checked and rechecked before top military officials of the two countries signed the documents pertaining to the LoC which were thereafter approved by the governments of India and Pakistan.

It was a lengthy and exhaustive process that led to the delineation of the LoC. As many as nine meetings were held between the senior military commanders of the two countries and their teams between August 10, 1972 and December 11, 1972. The military commanders of the two countries alternated between Suchetgarh near Jammu on the Indian side and Wagah checkpost on the Pakistani side as venues for the LoC talks. At each meeting, the inputs of sub-sectors were discussed and the thorny points resolved.

The delineation of the LoC was effected during nine meetings as follows :

	Dates	*Venue*
(a) First meeting	Aug, 10-12 1972	Suchetgarh
(b) Second meeting	Aug, 21-22 1972	Wagah
(c) Third meeting	Aug, 28-29 1972	Suchetgarh
(d) Fourth meeting	September, 3-15 1972	Wagah
(e) Fifth meeting	Sept 18 - Oct 1, 1972	Suchetgarh
(f) Sixth meeting	Oct 7-8, 1972	Wagah
(g) Seventh meeting	Oct 14-22, 1972	Suchetgarh
(h) Eighth meeting	Nov 7-9, 1972	Wagah
(i) Ninth and final meeting	December 11, 1972	Suchetgarh

On many occasions, to resolve a dispute, a joint survey was ordered to ensure that nothing was left vague or uncertain. To resolve some contentious issues, the Army Chiefs of India and Pakistan had held several meetings at Lahore in November and December 1972. The meetings between Field Marshal Sam Mankshaw and General Tikka Khan ensured that all issues were amicably resolved.

India and Pakistan had very carefully selected senior military commanders to carry out the historic task of delineation of the LoC. This was in the wake of the Simla Agreement of July 2, 1972 which stipulated that in Jammu and Kashmir, the LoC separating the two Armies on the day of ceasefire will be delineated.

The Indian side was led by the highly decorated soldier, Lt Gen P S Bhagat, while his Pakistani counterpart was an equally distinguished soldier, Lt Gen Hameed Khan. Both knew each other since their days in the Indian Military Academy, Dehradun.

Gen Bhagat's team included the then Director Military Operations, Maj Gen I S Gill, while his Pakistani counterpart, the then Director Military Operations, Brig S M Abbasi, a member of the princely family of Bahawalpur, represented his country. Deputy Directors of Survey of India and Pakistan were also represented, along with a number of trained survey personnel who were armed with survey equipment.

The composition of the two delegations was as under :

Indian Delegation	*Pakistan Delegation*
Lt Gen P S Bhagat	Lt Gen Abdul Hameed Khan
Maj Gen M R Rajwade	Brig S M Abbasi
Maj Gen I S Gill	Col Mahmud Shaukat
Col C M Sahni	Col Syed Refaqat
Lt Col M S Chahal	Lt Col M M Afzal Khan
Lt Col B M Tewari	Lt Col Ahmad Saeed

The senior military commanders of the two sides were assisted by three sector commanders along the entire length of 740 km-long LoC which was divided in three segments—the Southern Sector, the Central Sector and the Northern Sector. In turn, sector commanders were assisted by sub-sector commanders of Paratpur sub-sector, Kargil sub-sector (including Batalik), Shingo (Kaksar) sub-sector and Dras sub-sector—the areas of the Kargil conflict.

During this entire laborious, time-consuming exercise, the LoC was reproduced on two sets of maps prepared by each side, each set consisting of 27 map sheets formed into 19 mosaics. Each individual mosaic of all four sets of maps with the Line of Control marked on them was signed by the two countries' military commanders and each side exchanged one set of signed mosaics as required under the joint statement by the representatives of

Government of India and Pakistan signed at New Delhi on August 29, 1972.

This clearly delineated the LoC, which starts at Sangam and ends at Point NJ 9842:

Apart from the maps, there were 19 annexures, consisting of 40 pages, giving the details of every feature and landmark of the LoC. The delineated LoC was thus jointly prepared and signed by two senior military commanders and exchanged on December 11, 1972 at Suchetgarh.

Immediately after signing of the delineation maps and documents at the final meeting of military commanders on December 11, 1972, the Indian Director of Military Operations flew to New Delhi and reported to the Army Chief that the task had finally been completed. He carried with him copies of the signed delineation proceedings and one copy of the maps signed at 1500 hours on December 11, 1972.

The Army Chief presented these documents at a meeting of the Political Affairs Committee of the Cabinet at 1600 hours the same day.

At 1620 hours, a message was received from Pakistan President Special Assistant, Aziz Ahmed to Indian Prime Minister's Principal Secretary, P N Haksar. The message said that the government of Pakistan had accorded its approval to the joint recommendations submitted by the military commanders of the two countries on that day regarding the delineation of the LoC in Jammu and Kashmir.

This message was passed to the Army Chief at Parliament House and at 1747 hours, the Indian DMO informed his Pakistani counterpart over phone that the government of India also had accorded its approval to the joint recommendations.

At 0700 hours on December 17, 1972, the mutually agreed statement was released in New Delhi and Islamabad simultaneously. At 2100 hours on December 20, 1972, a joint statement by the Indian and Pakistan governments was released to the media regarding withdrawal of troops to the International Border and the LoC.

It is surprising that for a period of 27 years, the sanctity of the LoC was never questioned by Pakistan. A pertinent paragraph of the Simla Agreement, dwelling on the sanctity of the LoC, is quoted below :

"In order to initiate the process of the establishment of durable peace, both the governments agree that : in Jammu and Kashmir, the Line of Control resulting from ceasefire on 17th December, 1971 shall be respected by both sides without prejudice to the recognised position of either side. Neither side shall seek to alter it unilaterally, irrespective of mutual differences and legal interpretations. Both sides undertake to refrain from threat or use of force in violation of this Line.

Not that during the December 1972-May 1999 period, there were no clashes between the Armies of India and Pakistan on the LoC. Exchange of fire on the LoC has been frequent. Some times the clashes have been very serious. But every time the matter was amicably resolved at flag meetings of the two sides.

But the authenticity of the LoC was never questioned by Pakistan. In fact, the flag meetings used to be extremely cordial. As Lt Gen (Retd) Dr M L Chibber, who was Deputy Director of Military Operations after 1971 war and later C-in-C of Northern Command when Pakistan was prevented from occupying Soltoro Ridge and Siachen Glacier, has gone on record, saying that "Each flag meeting invariably developed into a competition in hospitality !"

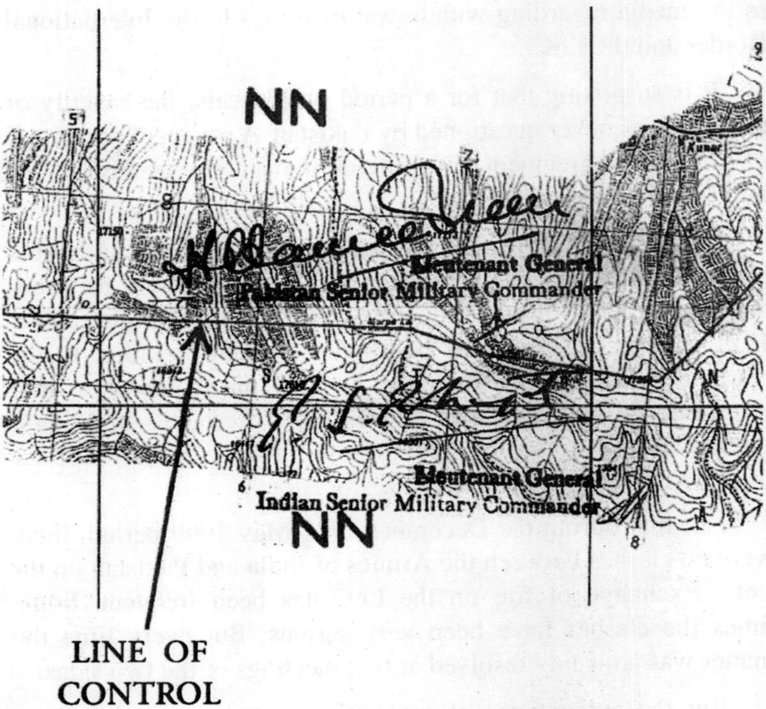

Delineation of the Line of Control in Jammu and Kashmir resulting from the cease fire of 17 December 1971 in accordance with paragraph 4 (II) of the Simla Agreement of 2 July 1972.

PART II

PAKISTAN : A ROGUE STATE ?

5 PAKISTAN ARMY

Pakistan is a State in search of an identity. The same can be said about its defence and security services, particularly ıe Pakistan Army.

The Kargil conflict turned the spotlight on the Pakistan Army. : was the first time in two decades when the notorious and biquotous Inter Services Intelligence (ISI) was overshadowed y "Big Brother"—Pak Army.

Discussed below are some important aspects of the Pakistan ırmy, such as its combat potential, its nexus with the notorious SI, Muslim fundamentalist outfits and, more importantly, its over-rowing Islamisation.

Pakistan Army comprises of nine Corps and Force Command Iorthern Area (FCNA). These contain 22 divisions, 15 ıdependent brigades (6 armoured and 9 infantry), 9 Corps artillery rigades, 7 engineering brigades and 15 army aviation squadrons. 'he aviation squadrons include two of attack helicopters.

Over and above all this, the Pakistan Army has eight air efence brigades. Pakistan's two principal fighting formations re Army Reserve North and Army Reserve South.

(Incidentally, the Indian Army consists of 11 Corps with a ›tal of 36 divisions and a number of independent brigades. The ıdian army has three Strike corps -- 1 Corps, 2 Corps and 21 'orps-- while the rest are holding corps. Each of the Strike Corps built around one armoured division. In addition, the Indian rmy has four engineer brigades and 14 Army Aviation Corps

Helicopter Units. The Corps of Air Defence Artillery (ADA) one of the newest formations in the Indian Army.)

Pakistan Army is a pivot for Islamabad's search for a natior identity. It is the implementing arm of Pakistan's pan-Islan policies and seeks to fulfill Pakistan's grand design of expandi its strategic frontiers by making inroads into Kashmir a Afghanistan.

It is one of the most professional, powerful and well-equipp armies of Asia, though it is also a fact that Pakistan Army, alo with the ISI, has several times virtually pushed the country the brink of being labelled as a terrorist state. Pak Army is know to be indulging in trafficking of narcotics and other crimin activities to raise money for financing covert operations in Ind and other countries as the tottering Pakistani economy does n allow liberal inflow of funds to the army.

When Indian Home Minister L K Advani had described July 1999 Pakistan as "a rogue state" (Advani was shown television angrily spelling out each alphabet of the five-lett adjective), he must be having the dangerous exploits of Pak Arn and the ISI on his mind. In democratic countries like Unit States, United Kingdom and India, it would be unthinkable f the army or the air force to be involved in such heinous crimes drug trafficking or export of terrorism. But Pakistan is a differe kettle of fish.

Pakistan Prime Minister Nawaz Sharif had created a sensati in an interview with *Washington Post* in September 1994 th former Army Chief, Gen Mirza Aslam Beg and former Direct General of the ISI, Lt Gen Assad Durrani, had met him with proposal in early 1991 during his first stint as Prime Ministe The proposal was for selling heroin to pay for the country's cove operations in Kashmir.

Sharif told the newspaper that he disapproved of the pla But he also admitted that he had no sources to confirm wheth Gen Beg obeyed him. Sharif later denied the story, but th newspaper stood by its report.

In 1993, Sharif had made a suo motu statement at the Neela Butt meeting that he had provided Rs 100 million to the Jamaat-e-Islami for intensifying the "movement" in the Kashmir valley.

In another incident, Gen Beg told journalist Altaf Gauhar in an interview published in *Politics and Business* that he had received a donation of Rs 140 million from Yunus Habib, Chief Operating Officer of Mehran Bank Ltd, which he had passed on to the ISI. He also said that the Army kept receiving donations from persons within the country and abroad.

The Far Eastern Economic Review and the Pakistani newspaper, *The Herald* extensively reported in 1993 of Pakistan Army's involvement in drug trafficking. It was under the ISI direction that American weapons and supplies moved north to Afghan Mujahideen by two principal means. One route utilised Pakistani Air Force transport.

But the main carrier of supplies was an organisation called the "National Logistic Cell" (NLC), the largest transport organisation in the country and wholly owned by Pakistan Army. All drivers and loaders were personnel of Pakistan Army. NLC trucks were used in the shipment of heroin from NWFP to Karachi port. These trucks were never checked by the police.

A CIA report of 1993 was explosive. It said that one of the top suspected heroin traffickers was Sohail Zia Butt, a brother-in-law of Nawaz Sharif. One of the six heroin gangs in Lahore, the "Takshali Gate-Hira Mandi" gang was headed by Butt. The report also stated that 13 Majors and two Brigadiers were involved in drug-trafficking cases during the Martial Law period under Zia Ul Haq.

The Pakistan Air Force also is not free from the drug trafficking charges. Sqn Ldr Farooq of PAF was arrested in New York in April 1997 by the US Drug Enforcement Agency for carrying two kilos of heroin worth more than Rs 20 million. A PAF aircraft, which was on a mission to bring military spare parts, was used to smuggle the heroin, hidden in marble lamps.

Interestingly, two months before the Farooq episode, London's famous investigative newspaper *The Sunday Times* had reported of links between Farooq and Asif Ali Zardari, husband of former Prime Minister Benazir Bhutto. The newspaper report quoted John Banks, a former British mercenary-turned American informant, as saying that he secretly taped conversation in which Zardari discussed drug shipments to US and UK. Sqn Ldr Farooq was also present at the meeting, the report added.

Secretary General of Bhutto's Pakistan People's Party (PPP), Ahmad Mukhtar, disclosed in May 1998 that the Auditor General of Pakistan had sent a list of 353 people to the Swiss Attorney General, requesting the Swiss authorities to investigate their bank accounts in Switzerland as these people were involved in drug trafficking with Asif Zardari. The list includes such big names as Corps Commander, Multan, Gen Trimzi, former Chief of Air Staff, Abbas Khattak, Maj Gen (Retd) Nasir Ullah Babbar, many Pak army officials of the rank of Brigadier and Colonel, besides former President Ghulam Ishaq Khan.

Soon after the Farooq episode, another PAF officer, Sqn Ldr Qasim Bhatti was arrested in Karachi. He confessed to the crime of running a 'sizable' ring of agents that had successfully transported heroin to the US on PAF aircraft on at least two occasions just before the Farooq incident. On one occasion, Sqn Ldr Bhatti himself carried heroin to a US air base.

During Gen Zia's rule, a PAF pilot was arrested for using the President's plane to smuggle out two kilos of heroin to the US in 1985. The contraband was hidden in the pilot's personal luggage.

Way back in 1975, a senior PAF officer was caught in Sweden on charges of smuggling through a C-130 transport plane.

The criminalisation of Pakistan has assumed such magnitude that even the national carrier, Pakistan International Airlines (PIA) became a conduit for drug trafficking. The practice became so widespread at one stage that some years back the Saudi Arab authorities threatened to stop direct flights between Peshawar and Jeddah.

ISLAMISATION OF PAK ARMY

The Islamisation of Pakistan Army started after military dictator Ayub Khan was overthrown and his successor Zulfiqar Ali Bhutto made Yahya Khan the Army Chief. Pakistan military leaders started quoting from the Quran and Sunnah.

The Islamisation received a big boost during the Afghan struggle against the Soviets. The ISI, which is the other side of the same coin, has always sought the help of fundamentalist parties like the Jamaat-e-Islami and organisations like the Tableegh Jammat and Markaz Dawawal-Irshad to serve their anti-India cause.

The Islamisation process in Pakistan Army went into the fifth gear during the tenure of President Zia. As a result, today most Major Generals and below are radical fundamentalists. Islamisation of the Pakistani troops begins from the day the recruits swear oath on the Shariat. This is systematically followed by periodic motivation on the basis of Islam. Such steady indoctrination provides fertile ground to Islamic fundamentalist parties in Pakistan to extend their influence over the armed forces personnel.

Besides, Pakistani troops are regularly subjected to religious tests which are based on the tenets of Islam as perceived by the majority Sunnis. These tests are intended to raise the level of religious awareness among Pakistani troops and ensures indoctrination.

Former Pakistan Army Chief General Aslam Beg unabashedly put across the role of Pak Army in his paper on "Defence planning in the era of strategic uncertainty" which was read on his behalf at a conference in New Delhi on January 27-28 on Asian Security in the 21st century. He said : "Afghanistan war of liberation experience provides the strength for the Kashmiri freedom fighter in the wider dimension of the conflict and should peace come to the war ravaged Afghanistan, the Mujahideen would like to pay back the gratitude they owe to their Kashmiri brothers for joining them in their struggle against the Soviet aggressor."

In fact, Pakistan Army has gone a step further than other armies by playing a pan-Islamic role. Pakistan armed forces personnel have fought in the 1967 and 1973 Arab-Israeli wars. The Pakistan Army has also fought alongside the fundamentalist groups in Kashmir in 1965 -- the period the flopped "Operation Gibraltar" -- and again since 1989 in the proxy war against India.

It is well known now that Pak Army soldiers fought in Afghanistan alongside the Mujahideen. In July 1999, at least 28 bodies of Pak Army soldiers were recovered from Afghanistan. President Zia had even offered to send his troops to Syria in 1982.

Having learnt its basics in Afghanistan and having trained over 25,000 terrorists from eight different nationalities, the Pakistan Army is today well poised to export terrorism and vigorously pursue the "foco" theory of the legendary Latin American guerilla leader, Che Guevara, which is now dominating the strategies of some states in North Africa and the Middle East. Focoism was based on the premise that a passive population could be aroused to revolutionary fervour by armed struggle of mercenaries. Guevara's was the world's first attempt to export terrorism and revolution.

The United States has been watching closely the spurt in Islamisation of Pakistan politics and military.

The US State Department warned Pakistan in January 1993 that on account of its alleged support of terrorist activities in Kashmir and Punjab, it was being put under "active continuing review" to determine whether it should be placed on the terrorist state list. In July 1993, Pakistan was removed from the informal terrorist watch list when the State Department determined that Pakistan had implemented "a policy of ending official support for terrorists in India."

The State Department terrorism report of 1994, released in April 1995, revealed a different story. It said : "There were credible reports in 1994 of official Pakistani support to Kashmiri militants who undertook attacks of terrorism in Indian-controlled Kashmir."

After six years of official silence on Pakistani support for terrorism in Kashmir, the Clinton administration is finally recognising the long-standing Pakistani threat to the region. This silence was broken finally in the last week of June 1999 when Washington came out openly holding Pakistan responsible for the fighting in Kargil. It accused Pakistan for exporting Talibanisation into Kashmir and rejected Pakistani lies about the invaders being "Kashmiri freedom fighters."

SPECIAL SERVICE GROUP (SSG)

The SSG played a pivotal role in Pakistan's incursion in Kargil. It was a tailor-made role for this elite unit of Pakistan Army.

A SSG commando is normally given breathtakingly diverse types of training—from snow training to mountaineering to para-dropping course, and even training in nuclear, biological and chemical warfare. Known for their aggressive but disciplined character and high morale, SSG commandos are capable of conducting high risk operations effectively under adverse conditions.

Pakistan Army had extensively used the SSG commandos for the Kargil incursions. This is evident from the fact that of the 725 Pakistani soldiers killed in the Kargil conflict, 68 were SSG personnel. Many sections of the intruders were led by SSG commandos.

The Indian Army had foiled a grand plan of the Pak Army for grabbing the highly strategic Turtuk sub-sector, located close to the Siachen Glacier. The ISI worked in tandem with the Pakistan Army in implementing the Turtuk plan. Turtuk has now been renamed as Hanif sub-sector after the Turtuk hero, Lt Hanifuddin, who laid down his life in a fierce battle that saw the Pakistanis driven out. SSG personnel had participated in a big way in the failed Turtuk operation. Virtually every single member of this 4000-odd strong unit has been tasked for anti-India operations and there is clamour for more. Pakistan Army is actively considering a proposal for establishment of a SSG Training School. Presently, the Commando Course is conducted on an ad-hoc basis.

Volunteers from regular infantry battalions and para-military forces having aptitude for SSG tasks are initially screened and imparted strenuous training at Cherat in Pakistan Occupied Kashmir (POK) where SSG's headquarters are located.

Those who qualify the various tests with distinction or high proficiency are selected and posted to various SSG battalions. Rest of the personnel are returned to their respective units.

The selected personnel, on joining their respective battalions, are further imparted training regarding their special task and familiarised with the terrain they have to operate in to maximise their combat efficiency.

Personnel lacking interest and those who fail to attain the requisite standards are also returned to their parent units. The officers selected for posting to SSG are physically tough and qualified in certain aspects to undertake specific operations.

The following table gives an insight into the various types of training imparted to the SSG personnel at different places :

Sl. No.	*Type of Training*	*Place of Training*	*Duration*
1.	Basic training	Jalooze Camp (near Cherat)	2 months
2.	Watermanship training	Mangla Dam	1 month
3.	Snow training	Kalam (NWFP)	3 weeks
4.	Mountaineering	Kohat/Cherat	3 weeks
5.	Weapon Training (Special focus on firing)	Cherat	2 months
6.	Explosive training	Cherat	2 months
7.	Paradropping course	Peshawar	1 month
8.	Navigation course	Cherat	1 month
9.	Test exercise	Sinkiari Area	3 weeks
10.	Tactical training	Surrounding area of Cherat	1 month
11.	Nuclear, biological and chemical warfare	Practice on dummy targets	not known

At least three of the existing four SSG battalions have India-specific charter of operational responsibility. The allocated areas of responsibility of the four battalions of the SSG are as follows:

* 1 SSG battalion—Jammu area and its dropping zone near Pathankot.
* 2 SSG battalion —Desert of Rajasthan.
* 3 SSG battalion—Kashmir valley.
* 21 SSG battalion—Not known. Available intelligence reports show that this particular battalion was training 30 Corps troops from October to December, 1995 in Sialkot. Some officers and Junior Commissioned Officers visit the areas of their operational responsibilities near the border once a year.

  Latest intelligence reports talked of deployment of unidentified companies of 2 and 3 SSG battalions in the following pattern :

- Three companies of 2 SSG battalion located at Karachi.
- One company of 3 SSG battalion located at Para Training School, Peshawar.

The SSG has several specialist companies, of which mention must be made of three companies : Musa, Zarrar and Iqbal.

(a) Musa Company : A frogman company, having expertise to carry out under-water operations. The strength of this company is about 80 personnel, which is less than a normal commando company. It also took part in joint naval exercise with PNS Iqbal in 1995.

(b) Zarrar Company : Its task is mainly anti-hijacking and anti-terrorism operations. Its personnel are issued gas masks. It is pertinent to note here that several gas masks were recovered from the Pakistani intruders in Kargil after their eviction. Personnel of this company are deployed in Karachi to assist in the handling of MQM situation. The strength of this company is 150.

(c) Iqbal Company : Basically a signal communication company, its personnel are trained in commando course, para-jumping and crypto. Its personnel use Type 77 wireless sets which have a range of 30 kms. A platoon is given to each commando battalion.

The SSG has a remarkable air-borne capability. It has some C-130 transport aircraft at its disposal. As many as 64 commandos can be para-dropped in 11 seconds.

The SSG uses the Puma, MI8 and HU1 helicopters for heliborne operations. Their capacities vary from five to 20 paratroopers.

Paradropping is done from an altitude varying from 700 feet to 1300 feet and the parachute is buried after drop in actual operations. Each individual carries 50 pounds of load which includes seven days of ration. A section of this unit carries one Rocket Propelled Grenade—RPG-7.

The role of the SSG personnel is clearly defined. Their peace time role is to curb the activities of terrorists and kidnapping activities and to maintain law and order situation in disturbed areas. They also deal with anti-hijacking and anti-insurgency operations. Their war time role is to destroy army installations, oil dumps, air fields, bridges, TV and Radio stations, power grids, radar stations and ships and capture of VIPs and senior officers.

A SSG commando gets many incentives which are not given to ordinary Pakistani soldiers. The SSG personnel get 30 per cent more of their basic pay. Besides, they get para and commando allowances and a special combat dress.

The SSG has a naval wing also, known as SSG (N). Pakistan Navy has a SSG unit. Its personnel are trained as commandos, frogmen and paratroopers for clandestine operations, such as underwater sabotage, laying of mines in the approaches to harbours and destruction of vital communication links, ammunition depots, ships and offshore oil terminals.

The underwater craft of the Pak Navy are manned by the SSG(N) personnel and are placed under the operational control of PNS Iqbal. The network of smugglers and ISI operatives working in tandem, landing men and material in support of their subversive element ashore, is likely to be exploited by the SSG(N) during war.

NORTHERN LIGHT INFANTRY (NLI)

One of the lesser-known facts of Pakistan's misadventure in Kargil is that it used mainly Kashmiri fighting units from Pakistan Occupied Kashmir and the Centrally administered Northern Areas and very little forces from the mainland.

It was a tactical decision for Pakistani military strategists. Arrival of body bags of mainland troops would have created shock waves across Pakistan. Kashmiri fighting forces, such as Northern Light Infantry (NLI), can be used freely and even as cannon fodder, as indeed the NLI personnel were eventually used.

Moreover, for Pakistan it was a battle for "liberation of Kashmir". So it was in the fitness of things that Kashmiri units were used. And of course, there was the operational reason for inducting NLI personnel into the Kargil war theater in view of their expertise in high altitude warfare and their natural acclimatisation for fighting at glaciated heights.

Pakistan has a chequered history of trouble in Northern Areas and the POK, which they call the "Azad Kashmir". Soon after its independence, Pakistan had split the POK into two parts—"Azad Kashmir" and Northern Areas.

People in Northern Areas have no constitutional, legal or political rights. The territory is ruled by an Administrator thrust on the locals by Islamabad. The Administrator is viewed as an "outsider" and an "agent" of the Central Government who does not understand the problems of the locals. The Administrator neither has the time nor the inclination to address the endless problems of the locals.

There is no legislative assembly or Supreme Court or hospitals or medical colleges or universities in the Northern Areas which the POK boasts of. Even after fifty years of direct rule from

Islamabad, the infrastructural "facilities" in Northern Areas are of medieval times. Metalled roads, good schools or even dispensaries are still viewed by the local inhabitants as luxuries.

This situation has given rise to sporadic troubles and unrest. A local Senior Superintendent of Police (SSP), Hamir Hamza, had raised the banner of revolt some years ago, demanding, among other things, more judicial, political and constitutional freedom. He was suspended and thrown behind the bars. He fought his way right upto the Pakistani Supreme Court and got himself reinstated.

Gilgit and Skardu-- which figured prominently during the Kargil conflict -- are parts of the Northern Areas. The main towns of POK are Muzaffarabad, the "so-called" capital of "Azad Kashmir", and Mirpur.

The sectarian break-up in the Northern Areas consists of eight major ethnic groups -- the Baltees, Shins, Yashkums, Mughals, Kashmiris, Pathans, Ladakhis and Turks who speak dialects on Balti, Shina, Brushaki, Khawer, Wakhi, Turki, Tibetan, Pushto, Urdu and Persian.

The Northern Areas, despite a very small population presents a very diverse sectarian picture, with the presence of four Muslim sects --Shia, Sunni, Ismails and Nubakshshies.

During 1880s, following the annexation of the North West Frontier Province (NWFP) and extension of the British military control upto the Durand Line, the British were required to manage the tribals in NWFP. Due to manifold problems -- including ignorance of terrain, language, customs and habits of hostile tribals-- the Indian and British units could not be used in isolation.

Therefore, the Pakistan militia and Scout units were raised by recruiting local tribals. These units were employed in front and on the flanks for gathering information and protection. Later, the role of militia/scouts was changed to picqueting and guarding of routes well before the military force could be launched or employed.

Consequent to the creation of Pakistan in 1947, the militia and Scouts were gradually reorganised and equipped with modern weapons. Army units were withdrawn and militia scouts deployed in POK, NWFP and Baluchistan

DIG, Northern Area, Gilgit and following Scouts were deployed in POK : (i) Karakoram Scouts, headquarters at Skardu; (ii) Northern Scouts, headquarters at South Gilgit; and (iii) Gilgit Scouts, headquarters at North Gilgit.

During 1973, HQ Northern Scouts alongwith its Scout wings Karakoram Scouts, Northern Scouts and Gilgit Scouts were reorganised as Northern Light Infantry (NLI) battalions.

On raising, the NLI battalions were placed under the control of Pakistan's Ministry of Defence. The regimental centre of NLI battalions was located at Bunji near Gilgit.

The area-wise proportion of recruitment in NLI battalions is as follows : Gilgit (55 per cent), Balistan (35 %), Others, including Gircha, Chilas and POK (10 %).

Shias form the chunk of the NLI battalions with 49 per cent in the ethnic composition of NLI battalions, followed by Ismailees (23 %), Sunnis (18 %) and Noor Bakshish (10 %). The ethnic pattern in NLI Mortar Batteries is in equal proportion for Sunnis, Shias and others.

On reorganisation, ten NLI battalions, numbering from 1 to 10, along with three independent NLI Batteries, were raised. Four additional battalions were raised in 1985 due to employment at Siachen.

The NLI personnel have been trained in anti-heliborne, commando operations and snow warfare. The commando trained personnels are also deputed to Special Service Group (SSG).

The NLI personnel are capable of :

(i) Closing with the enemy by means of fire and manoeuvre in order to destroy him.

(ii) Repulsing enemy attack by fire and counter attack.

(iii) Providing base for fire and manoeuvre elements.

(iv) Seizing and holding ground.

(v) Conducting independent operations on a limited scale.

(vi) Participation in air landing operations when provided with sufficient air transportation.

(vii) Taking part in different types of operation by day and night.

(viii) Conducting operations in all types of terrain and climatic conditions.

(ix) Moving by any method -- cross-country, road, sea and air.

(x) Providing anti-tank protection.

(xi) Internal security and civil defence.

6 Terrorist Training Camps in Afghanistan and Pakistan

TRAINING CAMPS IN AFGHANISTAN

Training camps for militants involved in Kashmir, in battle fields around the world and in international terrorism are located in Nangarhar, Pakhtia, Logar and Kunar provinces of Afghanistan, bordering Pakistan and in several cases it is not clear which side of the Pak-Afghan border they are on. A majority of these camps were under Hizb-e-Islami (Hikmatyar) and Ittehad-e-Islami (Sayyaf) prior to establishment of Taliban control over these provinces. Pakistanis, Kashmiris and Arabs from Saudi Arabia, Algeria, Tunisia, Iraq, Egypt, Jordan, Palestine are among those being trained in these camps. International terrorism emanating from Afghanistan remains a major concern internationally, particularly to the US, which has hopes that the Taliban would take measures to curtail militant activities in areas under their control.

Al Badr-I and Al-Badr-II camps in Khost area of Pakhtia province are two of the major militant training camps in the country. Prior to the Taliban take over of Pakhtia, these camps were being run by Gulbuddin Hikmatyar. Soon after Taliban captured Kabul, these camps were reported to have been handed over to the Harkat ul-Ansar (HUA) for its use, after initial reports that Taliban had closed these camps. These two camps have been more in focus in past few years, particularly since a report by a journalist, Caroline Lees, who claimed to have clandestinely visited them in November 1996.

Camps in Khost Area

The Al Badr complex is the main training camp in Khost area. After the Taliban take over of Kabul, while the Al Badr-I and Al Badr-II camps in this complex were learnt to have been handed over to HUA, yet another camp was believed to have been occupied by a Libyan Islamic militant groups affiliated possibly with Al-Gama Al Islamiyah Al Muquatila, an organisation responsible for an assassination attempt on Libyan leader Qaddafi and involved in clashes with government security forces in Eastern Libya. The area occupied by Al Badr-I and Al Badr-II camps is believed to be a 12 square mile compound enclosed by barbed wire and look out posts. Al Badr-I holds, among others, about 200 Pakistani recruits at a time for training to fight against the Indian forces in Kashmir and for Harkat ul-Ansar. Al Badr-II has ground 160 trainees, mostly Arabs and Sudanese Muslims for the fight in Chechenya and Bosnia. They are taught lessons in bomb making, use of automatic weapons, rocket launchers and anti-aircraft guns.

Other camps in this area are Omar, Al Khuldan and Farouq camps along the Pak-Afghan border and known to be involved in training of Arab-Afghan mercenaries for fighting in Chechenya. The camp earlier worked under the patronage of Hikmatyar and trained militants for terrorist activities abroad. A training centre, called Abdullan Azam Training Centre for training of Arabs and Tajiks, also exists here. Camps affiliated to Osama bin Laden for training terrorists for Kashmir operations under the leadership of Egyptians and Afghans are also functioning in Khost area. Mine warfare training is reportedly carried out by the Egyptian militant group Al-Jehad at the Abu Bakr camp on the outskirts of Khost. Zhawar camp was being run by Jalaluddin Haqqani of Khalis faction prior to Taliban take over.

Some of the camps previously located in Peshawar are also learnt to have been shifted to Khost area. Qaida camp is one such example.

Other Camps in Pakhtia Province

Jali camp—known for training Kashmiri militants, and earlier linked to Ittehad-e-Islami (Sayyaf) group. The camp is also known to train Arab mercenaries for the fighting in Kashmir who are linked to Harkat ul-Ansar. A Syrian is currently believed to be leading the group of Arabs in this camp and was reported to be the main instigator behind the kidnapping of the four western hostages by the Al-Faran group.

Spin Shaga—a camp for Kashmiri militants located here was earlier being run by the Hizb-e-Islami (Hikmatyar) group.

Shepuli—a camp for Kashmiri militants located here under Hikmatyar's group is now under Taliban control.

Camps in Nangarhar province

Teraki Tangi—Kashmiri militants are known to be trained in a camp located here.

Nazian Shinwar—known for training Kashmiri militants and earlier linked to Ittehad-e-Islami (Sayyaf) group. The camp is also known to train Arab mercenaries for the fighting in Kashmir who are linked to Harkat ul-Ansar.

Muzaffarabad (District Shinwari)—Kashmiri militants were known to be trained in a camp earlier patronised by Hikmatyar and Sayyaf.

Dehbala—a camp for Kashmiri militants earlier run under Hikmatyar's patronage is located here.

Jalalabad camp—a leader of Egyptian militant group Al Gama Al Islamiya Shawki Al-Islambuli was known to have run a training camp for Arab mercenaries in Jalalabad for the Afghan Jehad. Arabs, especially Egyptian, belonging to the Al Game are known to be undergoing training here for terrorist activities abroad. The area between Jaialabad and Torkham along the Pak-Afghan border is known to be base of Arabs undergoing training.

Darunta—a camp run by Abu Abdullah, an Egyptian is located here. Approximately 300 mercenaries from Philippines, Pakistan, POK, Kashmir, Malaysia, Turkey, Egypt, Algeria and Sudan are known to be receiving training in this camp. Militants from here have been involved in fighting in Bosnia and Azerbaijan while a large number are presently in Chechenya and Kashmir. A training course on explosives for Arab terrorists was reportedly conducted by an Algerian here in early 1996. The camp is financed by Islamic terrorist organisations. ISI officers are learnt to be frequently visiting this camp.

A "Special Bureau" is learnt to have been opened in early 1996 in Jalalabad, then controlled by Arabs linked to Abdul Rasool Sayyaf.

Camps in Logar Province

Kanjak camps—earlier under Hikmatyar.

Camps in Kunar Province

Camps for training of Kashmiri militants earlier supervised by personnel of Sayyaf and Hikmatyar exist in Harikat, Pit Qala, Sarkanay and Pench.

Toshi camp, located near Asadabad, is a training centre for large numbers of Kashmiri fighters and is under control of Pak ISI.

A militant Arab group called Khalifa group led by Jordanian-Palestinian national, Abu Abdullah Al Refaee, is based in Kunar. It recently threatened to raise an Islamic army to wage was against the West. The group is reportedly in league with Takfiris, yet another militant Arab militant group.

The Ikhuan-ul-Muslimeen (Muslim brotherhood) is also active in Kunar province for consolidating their bases in the regions bordering the Central Asian States, especially Tajikistan.

Another Egyptian militant group Al-Jehad led by Islambuji has training bases in Kunar and Nangarhar provinces of Afghanistan and also a camp in Jalozai region in NWFP, Pakistan. The group receives financial assistance from private individuals in Saudi Arabia through the "Human Concerned International" organisation registered in Canada. This organisation undertakes social projects in Afghanistan.

Camps in Kabul Province

The Muslim Brotherhood is known to provide training to Kashmiri militants in camps located in Paghman area of Kabul province. There are also reports of a camp being run by Taliban some 15 kms outside the Kabul City.

A Services Bureau, a branch of the Peshawar Services Bureau, is in existence in Kabul and provides support to mercenaries, especially Arabs. The Bureau was earlier headed by an Egyptian called Abu Mohsin who had links with Ittehad-e-Islami of Abdul Rasool Sayyaf. An Algerian, Boudjema Bounoua @ Abdallah Anas of Islamic Salvation front and married to daughter of Abdallah Azam (the founder of the Peshawar Services Bureau), was in-charge of the Bureau till February 1996. Bounoua was responsible for training mercenaries of Algerian origin in Afghanistan to support Ahmed Shah Masood and is known to have an Afghan diplomatic passport. He was expelled from France in August 1992 and was found in Peshawar later in October 1993.

Camps in Badakhshan, Kunduz and Takhar Provinces

There are approximately 20 training camps in this area for training of Islamic Tajik rebels. A number of Algerians, Libyans. Egyptians and Chechens are in Kunduz province, undergoing training for terrorist activities abroad. The Muslim Brotherhood is also known to train Kashmiri militants in the northern provinces.

The location and affiliation of Khaled Ibn Al-Wajid camp in Afghanistan, used mainly for Kashmiri militants, is not known.

CAMPS IN PAKISTAN AREAS BORDERING AFGHANISTAN

Camps in NWFP

Al-Sada Camp (Peshawar), under Abdallah Azam, trained Arabs for terrorist activities abroad. Al Khidmat organisation, led by Sheikh Mohammad Abbas, is connected with this camp. The Camp Commander is currently an Egyptian called Suheib a.k.a. Abu Hashim/Isam. Hamas members from Egypt, Yemen, Saudi Arabia, Sudan, Algeria, Jordan and the Philippines are being trained at this camp. The camp is situated north of Peshawar. The trainees are referred to this camp through a letter written in the name of Al Khidmat organisation.

Al Qaidah camps (Peshawar), under Osama bin Laden, is a training centre for Arab militants.

Cherat Camp is used for training Arab Mujahideen. There is a Taliban Madarasa (camp) located in Cherat (Peshawar).

Teri Mangal—Training camp for Kashmiri militants is located here run by Hikmatyar.

Al Farouq camp or the Omar Ibn Al Khatab camp is close to the Al Sada camp, located about 100 km east of Khost on the Bapai Pass. The Camp is commanded by a Bangladeshi, Abu Amar, and Saudi nationals, Abdul Rahman, Amar Al-Masri and Abu Abdallah Al Yamani. About 250 activists of various countries under patronage of Hikmatyar's men are being trained in this camp.

Jaluzai camp is Abdul Rasool Sayyaf's training base in the city of Pabi, 20 km east of Peshawar. Activists are housed in Dar Al Argam hostel and a Madarasa which also serves as Sayyaf's Headquarters. Mostly Al Gama Al Islamiyah activists train here.

Parachinar, a training centre of ISI, is located at Parachinar Hills close to Jaji area of Pakhtia province in Afghanistan since late 1980s to train Afghan Mujahideen operating in various countries. Majority of the instructors are Pak defence personnel but some Arab speaking instructors probably from Sudan, Egypt, Algeria are also there. Mujahideen, belonging to various fundamentalist organisations around the globe and notably from Afghanistan, POK, Kashmir valley, Azerbaijan, Chechenya, Egypt, Algeria, Tajikistan, Armenia, Malaysia and Arakan hills of Myanmar come here for training in handling of arms, preparation of land mines and various type of sabotage, equipment from RDX, training in conducting of sabotage/terrorist activities, guerrilla warfare, commando training and hijacking of aeroplanes with the help of fake models of various type of planes. Maximum number of Afghan mercenaries are from among Jaji Pashtoons who are paid about US $ 300 per month for going to Kashmir Valley by ISI Chechenyan recruiting agents pay them US $ 500 per month for fighting in Chechenya against Russian forces. Recruiting agents of other Islamic fronts contact them either via ISI officials or through Hikmatyar/Sayyaf henchmen. A large number of Jaji mercenaries have also helped Azerbaijan army in their clashes with Armenian army.

A camp is located in the area of Khyber Pass. A Taliban madarasa is also located here.

A camp is located in the area of Bajaur Agency for training of Kashmiri militants.

An "Islamic Services Bureau" founded by Abdullah Azam in 1980, is located in Peshawar. It is actively involved in training of Islamic militants and providing logistics to mercenaries. The Bureau was led by a Jordanian Mohd Yousuf Abbas till February 1996 when he was extradited by Pak authorities to Saudi Arabia.

Camps in Baluchistan

Zizaral—a camp is located here for training of Kashmiri militants.

Sources of support to Islamic Fundamentalist groups involved in Militant activities

The Afghan Islamic groups receive support from Pakistan, Saudi Arabia and Gulf Countries. The main Middle East and Asian Islamic organisations, whose members train in the camps in Afghanistan and Pakistan include, the Egyptian Al Gama Al Islamiyah and members of its various factions, Algerian FIS and GIA, Tunisian Al-Nahdha, Palestinian Hamas and Islamic Jihad, Tajiki Islamic Renaissance, Chechen Mujahideen, Philippine Milf and Abu organisations, and unidentified organisations in Malaysia and Indonesia.

Several relief organisations and international humanitarian groups are instrumental in channelising funds to the Islamic organisations working in these camps. Most of these organisations have established their main centres in US, Canada, UK and other European countries. Most of these NGOs are grouped in an "Islamic Coordination Council" (ICC) located in Peshawar (GPO, Box 991, Peshawar, Tel 0092-521-45413, Telex-52383, IARAP-PK).

Support Organisations Involved in Militant Activities

Following are the support organisations known to be involved in militant activities in Afghanistan.

(i) Islamic Coordination Council : Most of the non government organisations in Peshawar and Afghanistan are grouped in it.

(ii) Maktab Al Kadamat.

(iii) Muwafiq Foundation in Peshawar : It funds Iranian propaganda material for Muslims in various countries and is itself financed by Iran. It also grants aid to Palestinian Hamas. This organisation also sends aid to Abu Sayyaf organisation in Philippines through Osama bin Laden's brother-in-law, Mohammed Jalal Halifa. This organisation was also involved in recruiting combatants and sending arms to Bosnia. It has branches in Jersey (UK) and Zagreb (Bosnia). Its representative in Jeddah is Qazi Yassin.

(iv) International Islamic Relief Organisation: It is a relief organisation of the world Islamic league (Rabitat Al Alem Al Islami), a Saudi organisation in Peshawar and Afghanistan. It maintains a camp in Kunduz for combatants in Bosnia and Chechenya.

(v) ISRA: It has close ties wit Hamas and maintains schools and clinics in Afghan cities.

(vi) Al Haramein Foundation: It is centered in Jeddah with branches in Pakistan. It has ties with Islamic activists from North Africa and veterans of the Afghan war.

(vii) Jammat Al Ahya Al Trath Al Islamiyah: Islamic Heritage Revival Association.

(viii) Jajnat a Bir Al Islamiyah: A Saudi organisation for refugee support.

(ix) Human Concern International: Head office in Canada operates in India, Pakistan and Afghanistan.

(x) Mercy International.

(xi) Masjid Al Aqsa Institute, Islamabad

Following are the Islamic organisations from Middle East and Asia, whose members train in the camps in Pakistan and Afghanistan:

(i) The Egyptian Al Gama Al Islamiyah and members of its various factions.

(ii) Algerian FIS And GIA

(iii) Tunisian Al Nahdha

(iv) Palestinian Hamas and Islamic Jehad

(v) Tajiki Islamic Renaissance

(vi) Chechen Mujahideen

(vii) Philippine MILF and Abu Sayyaf organisations and unidentified organisations in Malaysia and Indonesia.

7 MARKAZ-UD-DAAWA-WAL-IRSHAD (MDI)

Markaz-ud-Daawa-Wal-Irshad (MDI) was founded in 1986 with its first centre at Pakhtia (Zazi) in Afghanistan. The organisation gained prominence after its success in liberating Kunar province area of Afghanistan, from the Russian troops. It has not looked back after this operation and has grown manifold since its inception. During the Afghan struggle, Prof Zafar Iqbal, present Incharge of Markaz-e-Tayyiba came in contact with various people from Arab Ulemas. As a result of these meetings, he got the idea to train people for Jehad in Kashmir. He along with Hafiz Mohd Sayeed started this markaz at Shahadara in 1986. Later on, they shifted the institution to Muridke in 1989 to a huge complex in an area of 180 acres. MDI is instrumental in providing religious indoctrination and basic arms training to the militants from Afghanistan and has established itself as a centre of world wide Islamic fundamentalist activities.

Its headquarters is located at Chamberlane Road, Mochegate, Lahore, (Ph. 7231106, FAX-228894) on Gujranwala Road under the cover of Islamic Studies University. Its branches are at Lahore, Peshawar, Chelabandi (POK), and Muzaffarabad (POK).

AIMS AND OBJECTIVES

The MDI aims at uniting Muslims throughout the world through religious motivation; to fight against forces trying to weaken Islam; to extend help to the oppressed Muslims of the world; to spread and establish Islam in the entire world; to impart arms training and martial arts to the Muslims on the basis of Holy Quran; to establish Islamic government in all countries of the world on the principle that "Entire land of world belongs to Allah and the law of Allah should be promulgated in the land and that all Muslims must obey the orders of Allah".

Its aim in Kashmir is to liberate Kashmir and merge with Pakistan.

OFFICE BEARERS

Following are the office bearers of MDI :

Amir	- Prof Hafiz Mohd Saeed
Amir Hamza	- Editor Al Daawa, a publication of MDI
Zaki-ur-Rehman	- Chief (Amir LT J&K)
Hakid Mohd Sajeed	- Deputy Chief
Ammantullah Khan	- Chief of POK Affairs
Tanveer-u-din	- R/O Punjab, launching of training Centre, Jalalabad.
Mohd. Azam Cheema	- R/O Faislabad, Amir of Training Centre, Jalalabad.

MDI is organised by one Abdul Raha, a Saudi national.

MILITANT WING

Its militant outfit is Lashkar -e-Tayyiba (LET or LT) and its women wing is Binat-e-Jehad-e-Kashmir. ISI supplies arms under the banner of LET.

OTHER WINGS

Labour Wing—Located at Sialkot. Aims at cultivating labourers and lower level employees to join MDI. Once enrolled, they are asked to join Is!amic educational classes.

Students (Tulba) Wing— Located at Sialkot. Its cadres are drawn from Jammat-e-Tulba-al-Islam and recruits young students from schools and colleges.

Doctors Wing— Located at Lahore. Organises medical camps in Pakistan. Afghanistan and POK for medical aid to the common people.

Ladies (Masturati) Wing— Located at Lahore. Enrolls women for MDI. This group is yet small. The women are engaged in publication of MDI journals.

FUNDS

MDI is 90% funded by foreign countries and 10% by voluntary donations. The sources of the funds received by this institution is kept secret and the identity of the donor is not disclosed.

TRAINING

The MDI established its first training centre in Kunar province of Afghanistan in January, 1990. This was named as Maskar-e-Tayyiba, commonly known as Jehad Cantonment. It is also called Umul Quran. Volunteers from Arab and Central Asian countries as well as of Europe and Asia are also trained at this centre. The training is conducted over two terms ranging from 21 days to 90 days. The 21 days' training programme includes elementary exposure to weaponry and more emphasis is laid on indoctrination of Islamic values of life with special reference to Jehad. The volunteers found fit and willing are then sent for the second spell of training of 90 days duration which is conducted in a ruthless manner exposing the trainees to different aspects of guerrilla operations and sophisticated weaponry besides teaching them to withstand intensive interrogation using third degree methods. Pakistani trainees are permitted short period leave in between the two terms of the training whereas others have to undergo both terms almost in one go. Pakistani trainees were being offered Rs. 20,000 for opting to go to Kashmir but the amount was payable only at the assembling point in Muzaffarabad (POK).

The Commanders and instructors in MDI are primarily from Algeria, Sudan, Egypt and most of them have more than a decade's experience of combat in Afghanistan. Some of the Afghans have been brought to POK where new camps were built for them by the Pak Army. After training, Afghans have been sent to Kashmir, Algeria, Egypt and Sudan.

Its training camps in Pakistan and POK are as under:

Pakistan

(a) Beit-ul-Mujahideen, located at Akbar Street. Academy Town, Peshawar. Tel. 840656.

(b) At Islamabad, 99 Road, House No. 130, Section I-8/4. Tel. No. 445247.

(c) Al-Dawa-Islamic University, situated near Lahore, at Muridke.

POK

(a) Bait-ul-Mujahideen	-	Chelabandi, Muzaffarabad, serves as accommodation of LT militants.
(b) Camp Barakot	-	Apparently a refugee camp but used for cultivating and recruiting Kashmir youths.
(c) Maskar-un Al-Kara	-	Commando training is imparted particularly to foreign militants.
(d) Rajpian camp	-	Located at a distance of four

		hours from Muzaffarabad and focuses on teachings of MDI.
(e) Pakhtia	-	Located at a distance of one and half hours from Muzaffarabad. Ahle-e-Hadith mosque is in the centre of the city. Mujahideen and leaders look after activities of MDI in this town.
(f) Islam Garh	-	MDI spreading its activities in this area which is 28 Kms from Mirpur.
(g) Baranala	-	LT militants are very active.
(h) Lepa Sector	-	This is the major area of terrorist operations of LT militants.

ACTIVITIES

MDI is known to be taking active part in the ongoing 'Jehad' movements in Kashmir, Bosnia, Philippines, Myanmar, Nigeria and other parts of the world. Filipino militants have an office in Lahore and the expenditure for running it is met by MDI. A large number of Filipino militants have undergone military training in the LT training centres in Pakistan and Afghanistan. The fundamentalist leaders of the Philippines frequent MDI's Lahore-based office and headquarters and attend MDI's International Conventions. The November 1993 Convention was attended by Dr Mohd Ali and the November 1995 one by militant commander, Sheikh Abu Abdullah.

On January 1-2, 1995, the Filipino police arrested 16 militants including 9 Pakistanis and Anees Yousuf, brother of Ramzi Yousaf. The police suspected that these militants were related to an international syndicate of terrorists and were involved in hatching a conspiracy to eliminate President Ramos and Pope John Paul II. According to a report, there are 422 Pak nationals in the hilippines whose period of visas has ended. They are students nd belong to terrorist syndicates.

In May 1995, like-minded fundamentalist groups formed a Rapid Deployment Force' called 'Katiba Al-Mujahideen Batallion of the Mujahideen) at a meeting held in the Philippines. he meeting was attended among others by Al-Sheikh Abu Abdul ziz. Chief Commander of the 7th Brigade of Muslim forces in osnia. Salamat Hashan, Chairman of Moro Islamic Front Philippines). Abdul Karim, Chairman of Islamic Front (Eritrea) nd Prof Hafiz Mohd Saeed, Amir MDI (Pakistan). The meeting halked out four basic objectives— (a) nationalities and frontiers n the basis of races was an un-Islamic perception; (b) to work in upport of Muslims in all those parts of the world where action vas being taken against them; (c) the Mujahideen of the newly ormed Katiba Al-Mujahideen would carry out militant operations n tandem for promoting cooperation and goodwill, and fight in Kashmir to eliminate un-Islamic perceptions of nationalities and rontiers; and (d) Rabita Al-Jehad Al-Almi would not take part in ny campaign launched by people against their Muslim overnment in any Muslim country.

MDI's pamphlets and magazines persistently claim that MDI rranges terrorist training for hundreds of Muslims from abroad who then join terrorist movements in Kashmir, Bosnia, Philippines nd Eritrea. The number of aspirants for the training is increasing y the day. MDI publications regularly publish reports on activities f militants in the Philippines and Bosnia. Mohd Amin, a Pak ational and MDI militant commander, serves as representative f militants on the committee for external reports of a news gency based in Kata Bato in southern Philippines.

A vitriolic article by one Abu Talha captioned 'Kalma-al-Daawa', which appeared in the October 1996 issue of MDI magazine 'Al-Daawa' released on the eve of 9th International onvention of MDI, urged the people of Pakistan and all political arties to play their role in helping the Kashmiris to continue the ngoing Jehad and oust the Hindu Government in India. It declared that Kashmir would be liberated only through 'Jehad' and claim that the time for Mujahideen to enter India and fight the batt for 'Jehad' had come. LT, the militant wing of MDI, declar that after Kashmir, the rest of India would be its next target f 'Jehad' and that it was expanding its terrorist activities to over India.

MDI CONVENTIONS

The 8th annual convention of MDI was held on November 1995 in Lahore, in which its activists from Saudi Arabia, Indi Pakistan, France, Britain and Afghanistan took part. Th convention was particularly significant. An 11 point strate was announced by MDI Amir, which included—

(a) MDI would never accept division of Kashmir.

(b) Formations of Ulema Council for propaganda of Islam.

(c) All Muslim religious parts would be united.

Prominent leaders who attended the convention were

(a)	Hafiz Mohammad Saeed	- Amir, MDI
(b)	Abu-al-Wahab Anjum	- Commander, LT
(c)	Hafiz Abdul Salaam	- MDI Leader
(d)	Ghazi Abu Abdulla	- Chairman LT Kashmir
(e)	Sheikh Ahmad Saad	- Saudi Arabia
(f)	Sheikh Abu Abdullah	- Convenor Philippine Mujahideen
(g)	Abdur Qahar	- France
(h)	Maulana Shafiur	- UK
(i)	Zaku-ur-Rehman	- Amir LT, J&K
(j)	Ali Shah	- Afghanistan.

Significantly the conference was also attended by Qa Hussain Ahmad, JI Amir Pakistan. Abdul Rashid Turabi, JI Am POK and former ISI Chief Lt Gen (Retd) Hamid Gul.

9th Annual Conference of MDI was organised at Muridke in Lahore, from November 6-8, 1996 at Markaz-e-Tayyiba. Lakhs of people from all over Pakistan including forty thousands teachers belonging to various schools, institutions, universities and madrasas in Pakistan alongwith a large number of women participated. Apart from the Amirs of MDI and Jamiat Ahle-Hadith, delegates from 25 countries including Jordan, Britain, France, Afghanistan, Myanmar, Kuwait and Philippines also attended. Deliberations and speeches were marked by vitriolic attacks on India and Hindus were bracketed with Zionists and Christians as enemies of Islam. Literature was distributed to publicise atrocities on Muslims in Chechenya, Palestine, Bosnia Philippines, Kashmir and Arakan. It was disclosed that Jehadi Lashkars (squads) had been sent to these lands to liberate the Muslims there.

MDI elements in UK were engaged in recruiting elements for 'Jehad' in Kashmir and Afghanistan. Shahiq ur Rehman leader of MDI UK selected 300 muslims every year for 'jehad' training. Two courses are conducted: a three week religious indoctrination course and a three month commando course. MDI UK was also involved in procuring bullet proof vests, old maps of Kashmir and communication equipment/antennas for its cadres engaged in 'jehad'. Shahiq ur Rehman was sending Rs. 50,000 every month to Pakistan in the name of Kashmiri refugees.

8 SIPAH-E-SAHIBA PAKISTAN (SSP)

The SSP came into existence in 1982 as a reaction to the Iranian Revolution and increased Shia militancy in Pakistan. There is another school of thought which says that the phenomenon started from Jhang as a reaction to the socio-economic repression of the masses by Shia feudals in the area. Gen Zia ul-Haq has been credited with having nurtured the SSP as part of his Islamisation policy and as a response to TNFJ. The Saudi government also started backing the Deobandi school of thought and in the wake of Afghan war supplied funds and arms to Deobandi organisations. Indirectly, Americans and a few other western countries also supported the SSP to counter the growing Shia and Iranian influence in the region.

LEADERSHIP/ORGANISATION

The SSP is an off-shoot of Jamiat Uleme-e-Islam (JUI). Towns like Sargodha, Bahawalpur, Jhang, Multan and Muzaffargarh are the SSP strongholds. The dynamic leadership of Haq Nawaz Jhangvi popularised is campaign against Shias in their backyard, southern and western areas of Punjab. Jhangvi was killed by Shias in the late '80s. After the death of Maulvi Jhangvi, Maulana Ziaur Rehman Farooqi took over the leadership of the organisation. He was killed in a bomb explosion in Lahore on January 19, 1997

Details of the leadership are as follows:

Patron-in-Chief — Allama Ali Sher Ghazni

Chairman Supreme Council — Maulana Zia-ul-Qasmi

Chief	—	Ali Sher Haideri
Deputy Chief	—	Maulana Azam Tariq, MNA
Patron	—	Anwar Ali Shah
Vice President	—	Qazi Mohammad Ahmed Rashidi
Gen Secy	—	Mohd Yousuf Mujahid
Addl Gen Secy	—	Killed
Information Secy	—	Tariq Madni
Convenor	—	Muhammad Tayyab Qasim
Incharge Sect	—	Maulana Abdul Ghafoor Jhangvi
Patron-in-chief (Pb)	—	Maulana Ghulam Shabir Pasha
Provincial President (Pb)	—	Maulana Muhammad Ludhianvi
Financial Secy	—	Sheikh Mohd Ishaq
President Lahore	—	Maulana Abid Ali Qayum
Central President Lahore	—	Sheikh Hakim Ali
Student Wing Leader Lahore	—	Dr Haroon Ali Qasmi
President Faisalabad	—	Allama Tahir ul-Hassan
President Peshawar	—	Maulana Fazle Ahmad
President UK branch	—	Hafiz Abdul Hamid

IDEOLOGY/OBJECTIVES

Hostility against the Shias; restoration of the Khilafat system; protection of the Sunnis and their law Shariat.

CONNECTION WITH THE GOVERNMENT

The SSP draws support, inspiration and assistance from various political parties in Pakistan, mainly the JI and JUI. The JUI is associated with running a large number of Madarsas all over Pakistan from where recruits for HUA, SSP and Taliban are provided. Madarsas had mushroomed under official patronage during the regime of Zia Ul-Haq and although the Deobandis are in a minority, they have the largest number of Deeni Madarsas teaching 1,00,000 students in Punjab as against 95,000 in Brelvi Madarsas the majority Sunni sect.

AREAS OF OPERATION/MAJOR OPERATIONS

The SSP has influence in all the four provinces of Pakistan and was perhaps the most powerful extremist group in the country. It has succeeded in creating a political vote bank in Punjab and NWFP. The organisation has reportedly 500 offices and branches in all 34 districts of Punjab. It has 1,00,000 registered workers in Pakistan and 17 branches in foreign countries including the UAE, Saudi Arabia, Bangladesh, Canada and England.

According to Tariq Madni, Information Secretary of SSP, the relative sectarian peace in Karachi is partly due to the MQM factor as well as the administration which has largely dealt with both the organisations, the TJP and the SSP, in a fairly balanced manner, unlike the administration in Punjab where partisan steps complicate the situation. 'The government takes one sided action in Punjab and elsewhere in the country only to please Iran', he alleged.

Regarding presence of militants in party ranks, Madni said "we are reorganising the party with intention to remove the elements that have brought a bad name to the organisation by taking up arms which is not our policy. We have removed many like Malik Mohammad Ishaq, Lashkar Jhangvi (LJ) chief, who was a member of Central Shoora but took up arms because of the excesses by the administration." Madni denies any contact with the militant outfit LJ, "We have nothing to do with any such outfit. They comprise elements expelled from party due to indiscipline. Since they were trained in the organisation, have the same perceptions, they react whenever one of the former party workers fall victim to the sectarian frenzy".

According to the Chief of SSP, Ali Sher Haideri, the SSP :tivities in Sindh are on the rise. About 500 new members have cently been admitted to the SSP at Umarkot (Sindh). Recently, training workshop was held at Allah Wali Masjid on Khairpur oad, Nawabshah. During the address, Maulana Badr-ud-din ussain, President Sindh and Maulana Ali Haider Shah said that e Pak government was taking one sided action to please the anian government. It was decided during its general meeting at the party would follow 'Jail bharo tehriq' and surround arliament House in protest and will also disturb the mourning rocession of Shia community on the eve of Muharram.

It has been recently learnt that the SSP has directed its cadres change their names to Shia sounding ones and obtain national lentity cards on the new names to avoid being targetted by the ecurity forces. The organisation has also given a free hand to its ctivists to rob houses belonging to Shias and treat the loot as ooty'. Incidents of such nature have been reported in Karachi.

STRENGTH

The SSP has nearly 3,000-6,000 trained activists who indulge killing of Shias. Most SSP militants hail from Punjab and have eceived arms training from the HUA, Kashmir militant outfits nd Taliban on the pretext of participating in the Kashmir 'Jehad'. Iilitants belonging to the SSP and Lashkar-e-Jhangvi are reported have also obtained training by the Pak intelligence agencies.

FOREIGN LINKS/FUNDING

The SSP receives significant funding from Saudi Arabia hrough private sources in Pakistan. Prominent among them is Iunir Ahmed (Karachi) an importer of Islamic holy water from audi Arabia. The Saudi government is a major source of funds or the SSP and JUI. Funds are also acquired from various sources, ncluding Zakat, and donations from Sunni extremist groups. Drug noney was also reportedly involved. Other sources include donations through local Sunni organisations and trusts, schoo madarsas and study circles, contribution by political groups ar vested interest and funding by underground trade agencies.

The SSP has established a branch in the UK, the focus bei anti-Shia activities/propaganda. Activities of the group are carri out from the Mufti Mustafa madarsas, 11-13, St George Roa Forest Hill, London (Tel. No. 0181-471-2652).

Kadir Abbasi, leading the UK branch, works in clo cooperation with Maulvi Abdul Rehman Baba, leader of the Sau backed ultra right wing Sunni organisation 'Alami Majl Tahaffuze Khatme Nabuwwat', which has its office at 3 Stockwell Green, London (Tel No. 0171-737-8199). Most foreign funded madarsas (Sunni) in Pakistan are controlled the SSP.

The SSP has been linked to Ramzi Ahmed Yousuf's cadre terrorists.

PART III

A STATE WITHIN A STATE

9 INTER SERVICES INTELLIGENCE (ISI)

COVERT ACTION

Covert action is a regular instrument of Statecraft designed to achieve, through clandestine means, defined national objectives. Intelligence is not merely an input into policy but an instrument of policy.

The ISI is to Pakistan what the KGB was to the erstwhile Soviet Union — powerful, ubiquitous, and a state-within-state. A detailed study of ISI in this chapter will show how the agency has been Pakistan's invisible government over the years.

Clout of the ISI grew significantly during the Afghan war. The agency became a household name in India for its massive covert operations in Punjab in the early eighties and then in Jammu and Kashmir in late eighties. The ISI quickly spread its tentacles in large parts of India, particularly the north-east and the south.

The arrest of a leading Pakistani banker, Yunus Habib, by the Pakistan government in March 1994 blew the lid off the ISI's nefarious political activities within Pakistan. Habib came out with a stunning allegation that he had given Rs 140 million to the then Pakistan Army Chief, Gen Aslam Beg, for use in elections. Habib said he had given the money to the General before the November 1990 elections when he was the head of the Sindh office of the Habib Bank.

Gen Beg admitted that he had indeed received the amount but added that he had handed over the entire money to the ISI which spent Rs 60 million for election purposes. The General also stated that the ISI had been receiving donations from within the country and outside.

Interestingly, he said that the ISI worked under the Prime Minister and the President and was very categoric that the Pakistan Army had nothing to do with it.

More disclosures followed. The ISI chief during the relevant period, Lt Gen Assad Durrani, confirmed in a sworn affidavit that he had received the amount and had used part of the money for funding the election campaign of Nawaz Sharif and other opponents of Benazir Bhutto.

The cat was out of the bag. The ISI had been openly and blatantly playing a political game and had clearly aligned itself with a particular political party. And this when Bhutto had disbanded the Political Division of the ISI after she came into power in November 1988.

Obviously, the ISI had surreptitiously revived its abolished Political Division without the knowledge of the political executive and continued to act as the country's Big Brother.

Pakistan's former Air Chief, Air Marshal (retd) Asghar Khan, then wrote to his country's Chief Justice, Sajjad Ali Shah. His contention was that by accepting contributions from private parties, the ISI had tarnished the image of the armed forces. Pakistan Supreme Court Chief Justice treated Asghar Khan's letter as a public interest petition and took cognisance of the matter. Gen Beg said in his testimony before a full bench of the Supreme Court on June 16, 1997 that the ISI's Political Division was set up by the then Prime Minister Zulfiqar Ali Bhutto by an executive order in 1975 and the ISI worked directly under the Prime Minister, without the Army chief having any control over it.

Gen Beg's contention raised many an eyebrow within the country as the ISI's Political Division had been functional from the days of Field Marshal Ayub Khan, if not earlier. Despite this, the ISI used to take orders from the Army, ignoring the chief executive of the country. However, there was an exception to this when Lt Gen Javed Nasir was the ISI chief. Lt Gen Nasir had a running feud with the then Army Chief General Asif Nawaz Janjua.

A Punjabi of Kashmiri origin like Nawaz Sharif, Nasir's loyalties were with Sharif rather than Gen Janjua. Sharif continued to extend his patronage to Lt Gen Nasir despite the fact that the Pakistani press was full of stories how the latter was an anathema to Washington. The United States was upset with Lt Gen's close links with Egyptian terrorists operating from Pakistani territory. Secondly, Pentagon viewed Lt Gen Nasir as a major stumbling block in its efforts to buy back hundreds of shoulder-fired, surface-to-air Stinger missiles from the Afghan Mujahideen. Thirdly, it was an open secret how actively Lt Gen Nasir had been assisting such organisations as the Harkat ul-Ansar, which had been branded as a terrorist organisation by the US, and the Markaz Dawa Al Irshad.

This battle of nerves between the US and Lt Gen Nasir did not continue for long and the Americans finally humbled the senior Pakistani General. In January 1993, the US placed Pakistan in the watchlist of such countries which were suspected of sponsoring international terrorism. But this Damocles' sword dangled over Pakistan for just about six months when the US removed Pakistan from the watchlist in July 1993. The reason cited by the US was that Pakistan had taken certain remedial steps. It became known shortly afterwards what these steps were. *The Washington Post* reported on July 15, 1993 that Pakistan had agreed to remove Lt Gen Nasir from the top post of ISI and undertake a total revamp of the ISI by removing Lt Gen Nasir's hand-picked men from the ISI in exchange for taking Pakistan off the watchlist of suspected State sponsors of international terrorism.

Gen Beg's testimony focussed the world attention on the need to rein in intelligence agencies of the country which had become extra-constitutional powers.

Two comments of Pakistan's respected English daily *The Nation* during the relevant period are pertinent. The newspaper made an editorial comment on August 23, 1995 as follows: "Theoretically, the army has returned to the barracks, the GHQ has no role to play in the country's politics and the Chief of the Army Staff is a state functionary subordinate in the legally-constituted civilian authority. Nevertheless, we still hear of a troika meeting off and on to discuss urgent and priority matters of state policy and regardless of which party is in power, there is an undisguised endeavour in the elected representatives to stay on the right side of the Generals. Unfortunately, the country's politicians look towards the army as the real power broker whose support, they think, is necessary, to acquire power or sustain it."

Then, on June 28, 1997, the same paper commented as follows on the controversy generated by Gen Beg's testimony : "The case has re-focussed public attention on what is widely perceived to be a government within a government — the intelligence agencies and their virtual autonomous role in the political affairs of the country. The baneful influence of the intelligence agencies has spread its malign shadow over the political destiny of the country."

ISI'S DOUBLE GAMES

The ISI, like most intelligence services across the world, has pursued a strategy of double games, double-cross and double-talk. A classic case of this was the November 19, 1995 bombing of the Egyptian Embassy in Islamabad.

On that morning, a small car crashed through the Embassy gates and seconds later an explosion occurred on the front of the reception area where a crowd of visa seekers had gathered. But it was only a smaller explosion and meant to be a part of the diversionary tactics for a bigger and more effective one.

In this chaotic scene, a bigger vehicle, a Mazda van, speeded through the broken gates and exploded after hitting the main building. It was a suicidal operation and the van carried an estimated 400 to 500 kg of plastic explosives. Eighteen people, apart from the suicide bomber, were killed in this explosion. The Islamic Jihad group of Egypt later claimed responsibility for the baffling attack in the heart of Pakistan.

Yossef Bodansky, a respected military and threat analyst of the US and Director of the Congressional Task Force on Terrorism and Unconventional Warfare, has brilliantly analysed the hidden motives behind the Egyptian Embassy bombing in his book "Bin Laden — The Man Who Declared War on America" as follows :

"But the Islamists were guests in Pakistan — hosted and sponsored by the local intelligence service. Initially it did not make much sense that they struck out at the capital of a state that had been so hospitable to them and supportive of their cause. The facilities and camps of the Egyptians, just like those of all other international Islamists groups, were tightly controlled and supervised by Pakistani intelligence, the ISI. Very little could escape the notice of the ISI. The senior Egyptian commanders, many in Peshawar, Islamabad and Karachi for more than a decade now, had always had very close relations with the senior echelons of the ISI. It did seem unreasonable for the Egyptians to risk this relationship for a single bomb. And in fact, they did not risk it. The relationship of the Egyptians with the ISI dictated the selection of Islamabad as the site for a spectacular act of terrorism.

"Because of the ISI's close relations with and tight control over the Islamists, it was virtually impossible for the Islamists to plan, much less carry out, such an operation without the ISI's knowledge. With Pakistan under international pressure to close down the Islamist terrorist infrastructure, the Egyptian Islamists would not have made the lives of their friends and benefactors in the ISI, who fought for their survival and sought permission for them to remain in Pakistan, more difficult by embarrassing them. The explosion in Islamabad served to confirm at least tacit support from individuals within the ISI. So although the Egyptian Islamists had many good reasons to strike at Egypt, it was the interest of the ISI — based on the internal power struggles in Pakistan— that determined Pakistan and not a third country as the site for the bombings.

"The roots of the explosion in Islamabad can be found in the 'legend of the coup' against Benazir Bhutto. According to the official version, an Islamist group military coup was narrowly averted in late September 1995. On September 26, a routine customs check of an official car in Kohat, on the Afghan border, caught Brigadier Mustansir Billah and a Colonel in civilian clothes trying to drive a car full of AK-type assault rifles and RPGs into Pakistan. When stopped, Billah tried to call another Colonel in Lahore to confirm that the weapons shipment was authorised official business. The officers were arrested anyway. The investigation led to Major General Zaheer ul-Islam Abbasi, a former senior ISI officer recently nominated commander of the Infantry Training Centre at Rawalpindi. According to the official version, these two generals, along with Colonels Kiyalu, Zahid and Amjad were planning a coup for September 30. Using the wepaons Billah was trying to smuggle, these senior officers would have tried to eliminate the high command and declare an Islamist state. More than thirty officers were arrested in connection with the alleged coup attempt.

"In reality, the 'coup' was a setup, a purge of current or former ISI elements who had actively sponsored terrorism against the US. Both Billah and Abbasi had cooperated with and supervised Harkat ul-Ansar, Hizb ul-Mujahideen, and other Islamist terrorist organisations. They were deeply and directly involved in Kashmir operations. If they had wanted to, they could have acquired all the weapons they needed for stockpiles of the Kashmiri terrorists on Pakistani soil rather than trying to smuggle them in from Afghanistan. Billah was arrested delivering weapons from the Taliban to be used in deniable international operations. All the weapons and explosives in Billah's possession could be traced to US-financed supplies to the DRA and not to purchases of the Pakistani government. If any of these items had been captured in the course of a terrorist operation, the Afghans would have been blamed, not Pakistan."

BACKGROUND OF ISI

The ISI was founded in 1948 by a British army officer, Maj Gen R Cawthorne, then Deputy Chief of Staff in Pakistan Army. The Australian born British Army officer had opted to serve with the Pakistan Army after the partition of India in 1947. The ISI Directorate was formed through the bifurcation of the Military Intelligence Directorate.

Field Marshal Ayub Khan, the President of Pakistan in the 1950s, expanded the role of ISI in safeguarding Pakistan's interests, monitoring opposition politicians, and sustaining military rule in Pakistan.

The ISI was reorganised in 1966 and expanded in 1969. During the rule of General Yahya Khan, the National Security Council (NSC) was formed to coordinate the functioning of Pakistan's intelligence agencies. But the NSC is no more functional and the ISI is playing the role of coordinating the functioning of the country's intelligence agencies.

In its initial years of formation, the ISI was seldom in limelight. Its main function was confined to interaction with the foreign Military Attaches accredited to Pakistan and supervising the working of Pakistani Military Attaches posted abroad.

It was with the growing involvement of the Pakistan Army during the days of Ayub Khan in Pakistani politics that the ISI's role started expanding. The successive Martial Law regimes, beginning with that of Gen Ayub Khan, strengthened the ISI to the detriment of other intelligence agencies, especially the Intelligence Bureau (IB), which was marginalised.

The ISI lost its importance during the regime of Zulfiqar Ali Bhutto, who was very critical of its role during the 1970 general elections, which triggered off the events leading to the partition of Pakistan and emergence of Bangladesh.

The ISI regained its lost glory after Gen Zia ul-Haq seized power in July 1977. In late 1979, when the Soviet Union intruded into Afghanistan, Pakistan became a frontline state for the US and the ISI got a never-before boost. As Bhutto decided to cooperate with the US and other Western countries to contain the Soviet intrusion, the ISI played a pivotal role in channelising assistance for the Afghan Mujahideen.

The Soviet invasion of Afghanistan made Pakistan a country of paramount geostrategic importance. In a matter of days, the US offered to reopen aid and military assistance to this "frontline state". For the remainder of Gen Zia's tenure, the US generally ignored Pakistan's developing nuclear programme.

By now, the ISI had acquired a halo of Pakistan's top national security agency. It monitored the activities of and provided advice and support to the Mujahideen and along with SSG commandos of the Pakistan Army helped guide the operations inside Afghanistan. The ISI trained about 83,000 Afghan Mujahideen between 1983 and 1997 and dispatched them to Afghanistan.

This action of the ISI, however, did not pass off without harm to Pakistan. Afghan and Soviet forces conducted raids against Mujahideen bases inside Pakistan and a campaign of terror bombings and sabotage was unleashed in Pakistani cities. These terror campaigns, guided by Afghan intelligence agents, caused hundreds of casualties.

In 1987, nearly 90 per cent of the 777 terrorist incidents recorded worldwide took place in Pakistan alone. The ISI continues to actively participate in the ongoing Afghan Civil War, supporting the Taliban which has ousted the Rabbani government and now controls nearly 90 per cent of Afghanistan.

The ISI is tasked with collection of foreign and domestic intelligence, coordination of intelligence functions of the three military services, surveillance over its cadres, foreigners, the media, politically active segments of Pakistani society, diplomats of other countries accredited to Pakistan and Pakistani diplomats serving outside the country. Besides, the other charter of duties of the ISI are interception and monitoring of communications and the conduct of covert offensive operations.

The ISI has become a state within a state, answerable neither to the leadership of the army nor to the President or the Prime Minister. As a result, there has been no real supervision of the ISI and corruption, narcotics and big money have all come into play, further complicating the political scenario. Drug money is used by the ISI to finance not only the Afghanistan war, but also the proxy war against India in Punjab and Kashmir.

The Joint Chiefs of Staff Committee deals with all problems bearing on the military aspects of the state security and is charged with integrating and coordinating the three services. Affiliated with the Committee are the offices of the Engineer-in-Chief, the Director General of Medical Service, the Director of Inter Services Public Relations, and the Director of Inter-Services Intelligence. The ISI Directorate is of particular importance at the joint services level. Its importance derives from the fact that the agency is charged with managing covert operations outside Pakistan — whether in Afghanistan, Kashmir, or farther afield.

The 1965 Indo-Pak war provoked a major crisis in intelligence. When the war started there was a complete collapse of the operations of all intelligence agencies of Pakistan as these agencies had been largely bogged down in domestic works such as tapping telephone conversations and chasing political suspects. Ayub Khan set up a committee headed by General Yahya Khan to examine the working of intelligence agencies.

Due to its deep involvement in domestic politics, the ISI has kept track of the incumbent regime's opponents. Prior to the imposition of Martial Law in 1958, the ISI reported to the Commander-in-Chief of the Army (C-in-C). When Martial Law was promulgated in 1958 all the intelligence agencies fell under the direct control of the President and Chief Martial Law Administrator, and the three intelligence agencies — ISI, IB and Military Intelligence— began competing to demonstrate their loyalty to Ayub Khan and his government. The ISI and the MI became extremely active during the 1964 Presidential election keeping politicians, particularly the East Pakistanis, under surveillance.

The ISI became even more deeply involved in domesti politics under General Yahya Khan, notably in East Pakistan where covert operations were mounted to ensure that no politica party should get an overall majority in the general elections. A amount of Rs 2.9 million was spent for this purpose and attempt were made to infiltrate the inner circles of the Awami League The operation was a complete disaster.

Zulfiqar Ali Bhutto promoted General Zia Ul Haq partl because the then ISI Chief, Gen Ghulam Jilani Khan, was activel promoting him. (Gen Zia repaid the favour when after he seize the power, he retained Gen Jilani as head of the ISI after hi scheduled retirement.) Bhutto established the Federal Securit Force and gave it wide-ranging powers to counter the influence of ISI, but the Force was abolished when the military regime o Zia ul-Haq seized power in 1977. When the Zulfiqar Ali Bhutt regime was unpopular with the military and the President (as wa Benazir Bhutto's first government), the ISI worked in tanden with opposition political parties to topple it.

The ISI became much more effective under the leadership o Lt Gen Hameed Gul. The 1990 elections are widely believed t have been rigged. The Islami Jamhoori Itehad (IJI) party was conglomerate formed of nine mainly rightist parties by the IS under Gul to ensure the defeat of Bhutto's Pakistan People' Party (PPP) in the polls. Gul denies this, claiming that the ISI' political cell created by Zulfiqar Ali Bhutto only 'monitored' th elections.

STRUCTURE OF ISI

The ISI functions under the Ministry of Defence. It has strength of over 25,000 personnel and has its headquarters i Islamabad. Its responsibility, essentially, is to collect, collate an disseminate military and external intelligence and conduc offensive operations against India.

The ISI structure is explained by the following chart :

DGISI

↓

(Lt Gen Ziauddin, w.e.f. October 12, 1998)

↓

Additional Director General

↓

Deputy Directors General (DDG) (3)

↓

DDG (POLITICAL) | DDG (EXTERNAL) | DDG (GENERAL ADMN)

DDG (POLITICAL) ↓

1. Joint Int Bureau (JIB)
2. Jt Int Miscellaneous (JIM)
3. Jt Int North (JIN)
4. Jt Int Tech (JIT)

DDG (EXTERNAL) ↓

Joint Counter Intelligence Bureau (JCIB)

↓

Director (Field Surveillance)

Director (External-Political)

Director (External for Asia, Europe and Middle East)

Director (Attached to the PM's Secretariat)

DDG (GENERAL ADMN) ↓

Jt Signal Int Bureau (JSIB)

Jt Int-X (JIX)

SPECIAL WINGS OF ISI

↓

1. ISI Academy
2. Military Liaison Section (MLS)

JOINT INTELLIGENCE X (JIX)

It serves as the secretariat which coordinates with and provides administrative support to the other ISI wings and field organisations. It also prepares intelligence estimates and threat assessments.

Headed by a Director, JIX looks after general administration and accounts of the ISI Directorate. The Director is assisted by five Deputy Directors, handling administration, budget, accounts, transport and miscellaneous work. It is one of the largest wings of the ISI Directorate.

JOINT INTELLIGENCE BUREAU (JIB)

It is the largest wing of the ISI Directorate with about 60 per cent of the staff of the Directorate on its rolls. The DDG is assisted by a Director who has under him five Assistant Directors in charge of the subject of Labour, Students, Political parties, Anti-terrorism and VIP security.

In addition, there are three sub-sections dealing exclusively with the political and economic developments in specified regions of the world:

(a) Sub-section 1 — deals with India and the Far East.

(b) Sub-section 2 — deals with communist countries.

(c) Sub-section 3 — deals with East Asia and Africa.

There is also a separate Special Wing dealing exclusively with Afghanistan, headed by a Director. The Section has three sub-sections, each looked after by a Deputy Director, dealing with :

(i) Training and operations.

(ii) Arms distribution and logistic support.

(iii) Training of Afghan refugees and psychological warfare.

JIB also controls the positioning and functioning of the Pakistani Military Attaches/Advisors in missions abroad.

JOINT COUNTER INTELLIGENCE BUREAU (JCIB)

It is responsible for field surveillance of Pakistani diplomats stationed abroad, as well as for conducting intelligence operations in the Middle East, South Asia, China, Afghanistan and the Muslim republics of the former Soviet Union.

DDG (External) controls the JCIB for surveillance of foreign diplomats and nationals, political leaders and ISI personnel. DDG (External) is assisted by four Directors, as follows :

(a) Director — field surveillance and foreign diplomats and foreigners.

(b) Director — External (Political)

(c) Director — External for Asia, Europe and Middle East.

(d) Director — attached to the Prime Minister's Secretariat.

This Wing also has a unit called Inter Services Security Section (ISSS) which maintains surveillance on ISI personnel. Detachments of JCIB are stationed at Lahore, Karachi, Peshawar, Kohat, Rawalpindi, Mardan, Nowshera, Attock, Muree, Jhelum, Kharjan, Gujranwala, Sialkot, Sahiwal, Multan, Sargodha, Hyderabad, Muzaffarabad, Tulbul and Gilgit. These detachments carry out counter intelligence tasks, apart from collecting internal political intelligence.

JOINT INTELLIGENCE NORTH (JIN)

It is responsible for carrying out special operations in Jammu and Kashmir, including infiltration, propaganda and other covert operations. It is also tasked with collection of intelligence on Jammu and Kashmir. It provides training and supply of arms and ammunition and funds to Kashmiri militants to carry out sabotage and subversion.

JOINT INTELLIGENCE MISCELLANEOUS (JIM)

It conducts espionage in Europe, America, Asia and Middle East— directly from the ISI Headquarters, through agents and indirectly through its officers posted abroad under cover assignments. It also operates trained spies in India and Afghanistan to carry out offensive intelligence operations.

JIM is headed by Director (Operations) who has under him two Deputy Directors for operations in Europe/America and in Asia/Middle East. There are eight Assistant Directors of the rank of Majors in this wing.

JOINT SIGNAL INTELLIGENCE BUREAU (JSIB)

Its main function is to provide communication network for the ISI and to collect intelligence through monitoring of communication links of neighbouring countries, particularly India and Afghanistan.

This wing also produces signal codes for the use of Services. A sizable number of officers and men from the Army Signal Corps have been taken here. JSIB has detachments at Karachi, Lahore and Peshawar, each headed by a Deputy Director.

It is headed by Director (Technical), who is of the rank of a Colonel and is assisted by three Deputy Directors for Wireless, Monitoring and Photos. It operates a chain of signals intelligence collection stations along the border with India and provides communication support to militants operating in Kashmir.

JOINT INTELLIGENCE TECHNICAL (JIT)

It deals with technical aids for intelligence operations. It handles all the electronic gadgets required for ISI's intelligence operations.

SPECIAL WINGS OF THE ISI

ISI ACADEMY : It was renamed in April 1989 as "Defence Services Intelligence Academy". It is headed by a Deputy Director (Training) who is assisted by Officer Commanding (Language) and Officer Commanding (Technical training).

MILITARY LIAISON SECTION (MLS) : Though the MLS is a part of Pakistan's Ministry of Interior, it functions directly under the control and command of the ISI Directorate. MLS is represented by all the civilian security agencies, para-military organisations, Federal Investigation Agency and Passport and Immigration Directorate.

In addition to these main elements, ISI also includes a separate explosives section and a chemical warfare section.

Pakistan Prime Minister Nawaz Sharif took two major decisions to strengthen the ISI when he returned to power, though it is not clear whether he took these decisions on his own or whether he was coerced into it by the Pakistan Army.

First, Sharif created an Economic Intelligence Division in the ISI. This Division has been charged with the responsibility to collect economic and financial intelligence, to monitor the activities of foreign firms in Pakistan and to collect evidence of bribery and other wheeling-dealings by politicians and bureaucrats in signing of major contracts, including defence deals, with the foreign companies.

The evidence against Benazir Bhutto and her since-jailed husband Asif Zardari of their alleged secret bank accounts in Switzerland was collected by the ISI.

Sharif created the second new division in the ISI to keep a tab on the ever-increasing sectarian strife in Pakistan. This division has been given the responsibility of coordinating all activities and intelligence on arms and narcotics smuggling and terrorism.

ISI-SPONSORED TERRORISM IN INDIA

The BJP-led government of Prime Minister Atal Behari Vajpayee made it known officially several times that it was preparing a White Paper on ISI's activities in India to be presented before Parliament. The document was completed in the latter quarter of 1998, but then the government got busy with Vajpayee's Lahore bus diplomacy. Against this backdrop, it was decided not to go ahead with the presentation of the White Paper as the Indo-Pak ties were showing signs of improvement and tabling the much-awaited White Paper on the floor of Parliament would obviously vitiate the atmosphere. Besides, Home Minister Advani was not too happy with the draft and wanted more punch to be brought into the paper.

The Kargil crisis had not erupted till then. And after it did, driving the intruders out of the country was obviously a higher priority. Besides, by the time the reality of Kargil intrusions had hit the BJP-led government in its face, it had already been voted out of power (by just one vote), the Lok Sabha had been dissolved and preparations were on for the snap general elections.

Nevertheless, the statistics prepared by the Ministry of Home Affairs speak volumes of the ISI's diabolical role in India. Following are the indicative quantifiable parameters prepared by the MHA on the magnitude and extent of damage caused by ISI-sponsored terrorism in India :

* Civilans killed : 29,151
* Security Forces personnel killed : 5,101
* Explosions caused : 4,730
* Persons rendered homeless : 2,78,601
* Estimated private and public property damaged : Rs 2,000 crore.
* Estimated security related costs :
  (a) Compensation to victims, expenditure on displaced persons, border fencing, raising of local counter-terrorist forces etc : Rs 18,500 crore
  (b) Estimated expenditure on Army and para-military forces deployed on internal security duties : Rs 46,000 crore
  (c) Losses due to disruption of economic activity in terrorism affected states : unquantifiable

* Automatic and other sophisticated weapons smuggled into India : 61,900 (recovered only 47,700)
* High explosives, mostly RDX, inducted : 51,810 kg• (recovered only 43,700 kg)

ISI'S COVERT ACTION

Covert action is an integral part of the State policy and constitutes an approved instrument of Statecraft where political and diplomatic options prove ineffective and military solutions are too hazardous or cost-ineffective. For civilised, democratic nations, covert action is incompatible with established norms and contravenes UN charter and accepted international practices.

The Afghanistan war and the ISI's neck-deep involvement in it provided the Pakistani secret service a tailor-made opportunity to hone its skills in covert action.

During the Afghan war, the ISI officers got access to denied intelligence and technology, large quantities of surplus terrorist hardware and trained manpower adept in covert warfare. This was the time when the ISI developed strategic operational linkages at two different planes : with fundamentalist Islamic groups the world over, from where recruits and material help was drawn for the Afghan war; and with drug cartels, gun runners, underworld and smugglers in several parts of the world to finance covert activities.

With this, the ISI had pulled off a strategic and intelligence initiative which it was all set to demonstrate to India with amazing results.••

• The lethality of RDX can be gauged from the fact that only about 275 kg of RDX was used in the March 12, 1993 serial blasts in Mumbai (Bombay) in which over 300 people were killed, nearly a thousand injured and property worth more than Rs 200 crore was destroyed.

•• Pakistani and foreign saboteurs infiltrated : 7,125

•• Indians subverted and trained by the ISI in Pakistan/POK/ Afghan camps : 19,800

It is not for nothing that an organisation of just 25,000 personnel inflicted a thousand cuts on India and unleashed such a well-orchestrated terror campaign that a country of one billion people is still fighting a no-win battle even as the security forces are stretched to their limits for more than a decade and a half.

Unstinted support from Pakistan Army's logistic support base, other security agencies and administrative departments as well as low benchmarks of deniability and accountability sharply enhanced the ISI's covert action capabilities vis-a-vis India.

There were numerous factors that led to the growth of Pakistani covert action programme against India.

First and foremost was that the hitherto denied technology equipment of Afghan war and terrorist hardware was made available to "frontline state" of Pakistan free of cost with the crucial advantage of deniability.

Covert action had been tremendously successful in Afghanistan and there was no reason to believe why it would not succeed in India.

The US, too, had virtually accepted covert action as an instrument of State policy and there was no reason why Washington would adopt different yardsticks when Pakistan were to use this instrument in a much bigger way vis-a-vis India. The US had given extensive training in covert action techniques. Besides, the ISI had got a liaison leverage with intelligence agencies of the countries involved in the Afghan operation.

The Afghan crisis period also coincided with political, military and intelligence leadership of Pakistan slipping into the hands of hawks.

The clout of ISI had increased phenomenally in the aftermath of the Afghan war in which it had succeeded against a superpower.

The Pakistani strategists that they had already lost three wars to India and they still were no match to India's military might which precluded the option of going for a military solution to the perceived Kashmir problem. Therefore, bleeding India white through an aggressive and sustained proxy war was an ideal option to undermine the growing economic and political pre-eminence of India. Such a pre-eminence of India was perceived by the Pakistani decision-makers as a threat to Pakistan's integrity which emphasised separateness.

Now let us focus on the role of ISI in different Indian states.

ISI ROLE IN PUNJAB — K1

It has been nearly two decades now since the ISI took up in a big way the task of training, guiding and arming the Punjab terrorists, dangling before them the carrot of the so-called "Khalistan". It is another matter that the militancy in Punjab died its natural death not because the ISI lost interest or for any other reason but because of the effective border fencing in Punjab.

Militancy continues to flourish in Kashmir and the North-east, mainly because their terrain is such that the borders cannot be fenced there.

A number of Punjab terrorists, including members belonging to the First and Second Panthic Committees are permanently based in Pakistan and have been coordinating their activities of subversion in Punjab under the guidance of the ISI. Elaborating the ISI's role in fomenting terrorism in Punjab, Gurdip Singh Sivia, a leader of the dreaded terrorist outfit, Babbar Khalsa, UK, who surrendered in August 1992, revealed that in spite of regular interaction with the Punjab terrorist leaders, ISI officials took all precautions to conceal their identity. The ISI officials described themselves as Chaudharies — the seniormost would be referred to as "Bada Cahudhary", the juniormost would be referred to as "Munshis".

ISI's active involvement in training and supply of arms and ammunition to the Punjab terrorists is evident from revelations made by arrested and surrendered Punjab militant leaders and recoveries of huge arms caches at their instance. Sivia admitted that he had arranged five successful infiltrations from Pakistan into India of Punjab terrorists with weapons, sponsored by ISI during 1989. Before his induction into India for coordinating smuggling of arms from Pakistan, Sivia was briefed by ISI about new routes along Gujarat border which could be used for this purpose. ISI's role in smuggling of arms and ammunition to the Punjab militants was also confirmed by the interrogation of a key arms smuggler, Karimbhai Hasanbhai. The smuggler, arrested in November 1992, admitted having brought as many as 22 arms consignments from Pakistan.

Then there is the famous case of Lal Singh alias Manjit Singh. This top terrorist was the coordinator of militants and was based in Pakistan. He and a top Pakistani spy, Mohammad Sharif, were smuggled into India in November 1991 by the ISI in pursuance of a grand plan of Pakistan. The plan—Kashmir Khalistan Front, codenamed K2—aimed at balkanisation of India by forging strategic alliance among Punjab and Kashmiri militants and Muslim fundamentalists to spread terror to other parts of India.

The tasks assigned to them by the ISI included coordination of smuggling of arms from Pakistan, building up a network of hideouts and training of Muslim fundamentalist youth in association with activists of fundamentalist Muslim organisations like Students' Islamic Movement of India (SIMI).

Pakistan has exploited the differences within the Punjab terrorists. Commenting on the split in the second Panthic Committee, Dr Sohan Singh, who was himself a protege of the ISI, said after his arrest on November 3, 1993 that the ISI played an important role in creating dissensions among the members of the second Panthic Committee. The promotion of groupism within the different militant groups by the ISI contributed to a large number of deaths of militants in inter-gang warfare.

With the departure of leaders of the Second Panthic Committee from Pakistan and maintenance of low profile by Pakistan-based Babbar Khalsa leaders, the First Panthic Committee of Wassan Singh Zaffarwal and Bhai Lakhbir Singh Rode has gained prominence. Latest intelligence reports say that the ISI now trusts Zaffarwal than anyone else.

JEI continues to be a conduit for the inflow of funds to Punjab terrorists. The ISI takes extreme precaution in handling the Punjab terrorists on Pakistan soil by isolating them and keeping them in separate areas. Punjab militants' handlers observe such restrictive security that they do not even disclose the ISI's telephone numbers to even top terrorists such as Paramjit Singh Panjwar.

ISI ROLE IN KASHMIR — K2

After the Soviet Union withdrew from Afghanistan finally in 1987, the ISI had lots of free time and fertile brain. The ISI bosses opened a new insurgency front in India when they turned to Jammu and Kashmir in the late eighties.

The process of subversion and brain-washing took place slowly and steadily, but its unhindered growth made sure that the Kashmir valley, which was known as "paradise on earth" became a breeding ground of bloody insurgency; where for more than a decade children have been growing under the shadow of AK-47 rifles; where the people receive the news of militants killing security personnel or security personnel killing militants nonchalantly.

According to the documents prepared by India's Ministry of Home Affairs, the ISI has the following four broad policy objectives :

(i) Sustain Kashmir movement at minimal cost and force its settlement on terms acceptable to Pakistan.

(ii) To weaken India's potential strength and national will by hitting at its perceived "Fault lines" and to puruse the policy of thousand cuts".

(iii) To prevent India from emerging as a strategically dominant power in the region.

(iv) To render Indian borders porous and bordering states vulnerable.

The ISI has drawn up an elaborate plan— for action at different planes, such as political, propaganda, para-military and covert—to achieve the above-mentioned policy objectives.

Here is how the ISI has been acting to achieve its objectives:

Political Action :

* Project existence of a vibrant "Freedom movement" in Kashmir by orchestrating activities of the terrorists, Pakistan-sponsored politico-religious organisations and media manipulation.

* Bolster pro-Pak support groups, human right lobbyists, foreign Parliamentarians, academicians etc to promote secessionst cause.

* Float and sustain an overground conglomerate, inclusive of political parties, subservient to Pakistan and project it as "third party" to the dispute representing "wishes and aspirations" of the Kashmiri people.

* Cause disaffection and alienation among Kashmiris using the religious card, non-performance of the elected government and alleged atrocities of security forces.

* Create and exploit pro-Pakistan "front organisations" among religious bodies, students, youth, government servants, judiciary, bar, intellectuals etc.

* Organise agitations, bandhs and seminars both within Jammu and Kashmir and abroad to provide legitimacy to the secessionist ideology and achieve publicity mileage for the "cause".

Propaganda Action :

* Build up assets in the local media and finance them to follow pro-Pakistan agenda.

* Use terrorists to coerce into submission the otherwise recalcitrant journalists.

* Use Media for intensive propaganda against India and its security forces eulogising actions of terrorists as "freedom fighters" and highlighting activities of over ground secessionist organisations.
* Use Pakistan TV, Radio and special broadcasting stations like Sada-e-Hurriyat, and influence section of the international media to support the Pakistani position on Kashmir.

Para-military Action :

* Recruit, train, motivate and coordinate covert actions of various terrorist groups.
* Build up elaborate border penetration capabilities, raise guides/couriers and develop dumping and distribution mechanism to ensure uninterrupted supply of arms, ammunition, explosives, communication equipment and other terrorist hardware to the militants.
* Build up channels for financial assistance to militants and subversive groups.
* Control and direct activities of militant groups through an elaborate communication system with main controls in POK at Muzaffarabad, Kotli and Sialkot etc.
* Identify anti-movement elements, particularly intelligence assets and former militants, now supporting the government, to eliminate them.
* With local recruitment nearly stopped, induct large number of foreign mercenaries.
* Bring hitherto unaffected areas, particularly of Jammu region into vortex of militancy.
* Use terrorist threat to seek acquiescence of moderate political leaders, government functionaries, media persons, religious leaders, social activists and academicians.
* Engineer terrorist attacks aimed at communal divide and possible backlash.

COVERT ACTION

* Pursue the "Qurban Ali Doctrine" of the "inevitable balkanisation of India, identify the fault lines, carry out intensive operational intelligence research and build covert capabilities in targeted areas.
* Carry out low-intensity warfare in different parts of India with special emphasis on Jammu and Kashmir, North-east and Punjab.
* Target VIPs.
* Forge operational and ideological alliance of Kashmiri militants and fundamentalist groups with covert networks in the hinterland and international terrorist outfits.
* Use infiltrators from Bangladesh to destabilise north-east and cause disruption in other areas.
* Push counterfeit currency in the country through various inlets and use hawala operators to finance covert action programme.
* Embarrass India by internationalising Kashmir issue, projecting India as violator of UN resolutions and charge it with dismal human rights record.
* Emphasise strategic parity with India as a guarantor of stability in the region.
* Build and support anti-India lobbies abroad among Parliamentarians, strategic opinion makers, think tanks and OIC leaders.
* Emphasise commonality of strategic interests of powers like China and the US to support Pakistan and underplay its role in promoting international terrorism, drug trafficking, acquisition of strategic weapon capabilities through clandestine means.
* Intelligence encirclement of India by establishing covert networks in its neighbourhood.

* Diversion of substantial manpower and economic resources on security related tasks and making its battle against terrorism increasingly expensive.

* Tie down Indian security forces in large numbers on internal duties, thereby impairing their offensive capabilities.

* Cause demoralisation among Indian security forces through the casualties inflicted on them, pressure of human rights groups and strains and stresses of hazardous anti-terrorist duties.

* Intensify security related espionage activities, cultivate agents in and around cantonments, defence establishments, defence production units and research facilities.

* Establishment of high tech signal intelligence interception and intelligence communication facilities.

* Promote and abet terrorism in border states like Punjab, Kashmir, Assam and Nagaland etc and carry out subversive propaganda on fundamentalist and communal lines among sections of border population.

* Establish intelligence networks in important cities like Jodhpur, Kota, Ahmedabad, Surat, Baroda, Bhuj, Jalandhar, Ludhiana, Pathankot, Jammu, Udhampur etc.

* Patronise border smugglers and criminals and use them for intelligence activities as also smuggling of weapons and narcotics.

The points very briefly mentioned above, in fact, sum up I's strategy vis-a-vis India, not just in respect of Jammu and ashmir. These are being adhered to in letter and spirit by the ISI Kashmir; first, because the tactics had been time-tested and e tuned by the time the ISI spread its tentacles to Jammu and shmir, and secondly, because this time the stakes were much gher.

Because of the higher stakes, ISI did in Kashmir what it d not do anywhere else : induct foreign mercenaries in a big wa To help Kashmiri militants, the ISI, with the assistance fundamentalist organisations, recruited nationals of Afghanista Bahrain, Sudan, Saudi Arabia and Egypt, apart from Pakistan. 1992, the ISI inducted trigger-happy Arab guerillas in the Kashm proxy war theater during 1992.

The next course of the ISI is going to be induction of Talib soldiers into the Kashmir valley under the banner of Harkat u Ansar. And this is going to be sooner rather than later.

ISI ROLE IN NORTH-EAST —K3

By the time the arm of the ISI octopus reached the nort eastern India in 1990, the secret agency had become a pa master in the fields of subversion, sabotage and terrorism.

ISI bosses eyed the north-east to open a third front. K3 w the third proxy war theater planned in India after the encouragi results from the K1 and K2 experiments.

They perceived that the north-east insurgents, particularly NSCN (I) and ULFA, were in a position to launch full-sca insurgent movements with some help. NSCN (I) was giv assistance through the DGFI of Bangladesh (the Banglade authorities have their own reasons to provide assistance to t north-east insurgents) and anti-India groups like the Freed Party and the JEI. As ULFA was against the Banglade immigrants, it was difficult for the ISI to contact them throu the DGFI or anti-India organisations mentioned above.

Therefore, initial contacts with ULFA were establish through the Punjab extremists. In February 1990, Bhai Bhagw Singh Mokhal was sent to contact ULFA militants in Assa After establishing contacts with the ULFA militants, the ISI tr to bring the DGFI, the Freedom Party and the JEI closer ULFA.

As ULFA was finding it difficult to procure weapons through ıe KIA, it was looking for alternative source of supply of eapons. Moreover, there was realisation among the top ULFA ilitants that Bangladesh could provide the much-needed ınctuary to the ULFA cadres.

Now let us see how the ISI began to assist the various north- ıst militant outfits from 1990 onwards :

ULFA

Munim Nabish, an important ULFA activist, who was later ɔpointed as the resident agent in Bangladesh, visited Karachi ıd Islamabad during December 1990 and January 1991. He met n ISI officer named "Chaudhuri". At this meeting, arrangements ɔr the visit of senior ULFA leaders to Pakistan were finalised. abish admitted to his visits to Pakistan during his interrogation fter he was arrested by the Assam Police.

Chairman Arbindo Rajkhowa, Vice-Chairman Pradeep Gogoi, ieneral Secretary Golap Barua and C-in-C Paresh Barua and Iunim Nabish, the top brass of ULFA, went to Islamabad and ıe Afghan border during March-April 1991 to meet Afghanistan trongman Gulbuddin Hekmatyar, who promised to supply arms ɔ ULFA. Rajkhowa's diary and other recovered documents onfirmed this visit of ULFA activists.

The first batch of ULFA militants went to Pakistan in June 991 to attend a two-week-long training course in the use of ıortars. Since then a number of ULFA batches have received rms training in Pakistan. This has been stated in the interrogation eports of surrendered/arrested ULFA militants like Sujit Das, Binod Das, Pranab Barua alias Laching Phukan, Vijay Bora and bdul Hamid alias Dulal Hazarika. Col Farooq of the Freedom Party has acted as a conduit between ULFA and the ISI. Bangladesh authorities provided fake passports to the ULFA adres.

In August 1991, ULFA paid 4 lakh US dollars to Col Farooq o procure sophisticated arms from Pakistan. The interrogation report of Khamakhaya Prasad Rana alias Abdul Karim, who wa arrested on the Indo-Pak border in September 1992, reveale this. ULFA had also received 12 VHF sets and eight binocular as gifts from the ISI.

In 1992, the ISI put pressure on Paresh Barua, Arbind Rajkhowa and others not to surrender to the Indian authorities. I February that year, Robin Handique, a senior ULFA leader, wen to Kathmandu and held a meeting with Pervez Afzal, a Counsello in the Pakistani Embassy in Nepal. Afzal told Handique that th ISI would provide arms to ULFA through the Punjab terrorists ULFA was told that weapons would have to be collected fror Punjab.

At ULFA's General Council meeting in February 1992 Siddharatha Phukan (of pro-talk faction) revealed that as condition of help, the ISI had instructed ULFA to sabotage oi refineries, railways and other vital installations. In October 1993 Colonel Sajjid of ISI met the ULFA Vice Chairman, Pradee Gogoi, at Shaiman Hotel in Chittagong. Thereafter, the two visite a new ISI training camp in the Chakma area.

At these and many other meetings with different ULFA leaders, the ISI promised to supply arms and ammunition t ULFA provided the outfit : (i) promised protection to minoritie and attacks on the Indian security forces, and (ii) agreed t hijack an aeroplane to gain publicity. Another condition laid dow by the ISI for supplying arms and ammunition was that in th event of a communal flare-up, ULFA should side with th minorities.

NSCN (I)

In April 1990, NSCN (I) Chairman Issac Swu visited Pakista to procure arms for his outfit. He travelled on Bangladesh passports. He was contacted by the ISI through the Freedon Party.

In January 1991, NSCN (I) Finance Secretary, Khayao Hurey was arrested by the Indian security forces. He revealed durin his interrogation that the NSCN (I) had received one million Takas from the Pakistani High Commission in Bangladesh.

The documents recovered from Khamakhya Prasad Rana alias Abdul Karim, mentioned earlier, revealed NSCN (I)'s connections with the ISI and the Freedom Party. He also disclosed that both ULFA and NSCN (I) were receiving weapons from the ISI.

NSCN (I)'s weapons are smuggled from the Thai-Cambodian border. Intelligence reports indicate that the Pakistani embassy officials in Thailand are providing assistance to NSCN (I) and other north-eastern insurgent groups in procuring weapons.

Another intelligence report indicated that Issac Swu and Th Muivah, General Secretary of NSCN (I) met an ISI official, Sajjad Ali, at the liaison office of the insurgent outfit at Bangkok in February 1994. In this meeting, NSCN (I) agreed to impart training to the Islamic Sevak Sangh (ISS) activists at NSCN (I) camps in North Cachar hills of Assam and Garo hills of Meghalaya.

PLA

The ISI's nexus with the PLA also has come to notice. A document recovered in January 1991 from Biren Singh alias German, the Finance Secretary of RPF (the political wing of the PLA) revealed PLA's connections with the ISI.

Two ISI operatives — Nasiruddin alias Mahiruddin alias Dilip and Yusuf Khan alias Pradeep, reached Imphal from Bangladesh with a group of PLA activists in February 1994. Both the ISI operatives were of the rank of Junior Commissioned Officers.

There were more intelligence reports of the blossoming ties between the ISI and the north-eastern insurgents. A meeting was held at Chittagong (Bangladesh) on January 2, 1993 between Biku Sema of NSCN (K), K Basumatari of Bodo Security Force and Arbindo Rajkhowa of ULFA. The ISI was represented at the meeting by Mohammad Salim. The discussions centred around increasing the cooperation level between the north-east insurgent groups and the ISI.

Col Faruque of ISI met NSCN (I) and ULFA leaders in Hojai area under Nagaon districts in January 1994. Shortly afterwards, the ISI opened a new unit and selected educated young activists of ULFA (50), NSCN (I) (15) and Bodos (60) for the above unit.

As part of its policy to keep India in a continuous state of ferment and open as many theaters of proxy war as possible, the ISI has been vigorously exploiting for nearly a decade the ethnic and regional susceptibilities of the people of the north-eastern India. It has been using NSCN (I), ULFA, PLA and Islamic Revolutionary Army of Manipur to create problems in the north-east.

Suddenly, Muslim organisations have mushroomed like barber shops in the north-east and it is likely that these are getting support of the ISI. Intelligence reports indicate that the Joint Intelligence (Miscellaneous) of the ISI has been given the responsibility for providing assistance to the north-eastern insurgent groups. The DGFI and the Freedom Party are working in tandem with the ISI.

Col Farooq Rehman of the Freedom Party had recently claimed that he had been working in association with the DGFI Major General Mohd Nasim to chalk out and implement a blueprint with the assistance of ISI to disintegrate North Eastern India. The JEI is also associated with this plan.

At this stage, it is still not possible to quantify the amount in monetary terms of ISI's help to the north-eastern insurgents. But one thing is clear. The ISI help has definitely raised their sagging morale and helped them in procuring sophisticated weapons and getting their cadres trained. It strengthened the resolve of the anti-talks factions to continue their armed struggle against India.

The ISI factor has been instrumental in coordinating the activities of different insurgent groups in the north-east. There are reports of the Pakistan army officers supervising the training of the north-eastern insurgents in Bangladesh. Nearly three-fourths of staff in the Pakistani High Commission in Bangladesh consists of intelligence officers of Pakistan.

Highly porous borders with Bangladesh, the unprecedented spurt in the infiltration and exfiltration of people from the Indo-Bangladesh border and the tardy pace of work of border fencing are some of the factors which have made available to the ISI a situation on the platter that has the biggest potential of serving the nefarious Pakistani plans — of disintegrating India. Unfortunately, the Indian decision-makers, including the politicians, have so far failed to see the writing on the wall.

If the north-eastern situation were to be allowed to deteriorate like this, by the next six or seven years, Pakistan would find itself on the verge of achieving in the north-east what it failed to achieve in Punjab and Kashmir.

ISI AND MUSLIM FUNDAMENTALISM

Unprecedented spurt in Hindu fundamentalism since late eighties; political instability created by the assassination of former Indian Prime Minister Rajiv Gandhi on May 21, 1991; the demolition of Babri mosque in Ayodhya by Hindu fanatics on December 6, 1992; the subsequent communal riots in various parts of the country; the March 12, 1993 serial blasts in Mumbai and the subsequent communal riots — all these developments provided golden opportunities to the ISI to carry on with its subversive anti-India activities with the sole aim of weakening and balkanisation of India. The ground was fertile for the ISI to sow the seeds of communal divide.

This was the phase when the ISI proceeded with surgical precision to cultivate muslim fundamentalists. The ISI took full advantage of the fact that a new generation of muslim youth had emerged which was conscious of its numerical strength and political power, the perceived raw deal it had received in the Indian Union and the alleged failure of the police to protect the lives and property of muslims led a section of the muslim community in India to believe that the only way to survive was to fight back.

The growth of fundamentalist organisations like the Students Islamic Movement of India (SIMI), the banned Islamic Sevak Sangh (whose cadres have now been amalgamated in the newly-formed People's Democratic Party), the All India Milli Council (AIMC) and the emergence of persons with pan-Islamic loyalties are a manifestation of this new awareness among the Muslim community.

In the late eighties, the ISI arranged an interface of Lal Singh alias Manjit Singh alias Iqbal— a top KLF militant— some Kashmiri militants and the Pakistan JEI in Lahore. The ISI had by then started brainwashing Punjab militants that their goal of creating "Khalistan" could not be achieved without the balkanisation of India and that was possible only if they were to join hands with Kashmir militants and militant Muslim elements in India. The disclosures of Lal Singh and Gurdeep Singh Sivia of Babbar Khalsa International clearly exposed the new offensive worked out by the ISI. Police and intelligence records show that it was decided at the Lahore meeting that SIMI would extend all cooperation to Lal Singh in his operation from Aligarh under an assumed Muslim identity. Lal Singh and Sivia were among the important cogs in the wheel of ISI to implement this new strategy.

Lal Singh established bases at Mumbai and Ahmedabad with the assistance of fundamentalist Muslim organisations. India's Western borders were extensively used for smuggling huge quantities of arms and ammunition during this period.

The interrogation of Tahir Jamal, ex-President of the Maharashtra unit of SIMI and his confidant Saqib Nachan, confirmed that prominent SIMI leaders had been tasked to provide all possible assistance to Punjab militants and raise trained squads of Muslim youths in the communally sensitive pockets. Police and intelligence records show that Bashir, a former President of SIMI, visited Lahore in January 1992 and finalised a plan to dispatch Muslim youth from India to Pakistan for a four-week-long training course in the use of arms and explosives. These records showed that SIMI was also provided substantial funds through hawala transactions to finance this operation.

Around this time, another muslim youth, Shoab Mohammad Ebrahim Mullah, fell in the police net. His interrogation confirmed that Indian muslim youth were sent to Pakistan for training in handling the latest armaments, including anti-aircraft guns.

The arrest of two Kashmiri Muslims in Hyderabad in November 1993 disclosed that Muslim youth from Hyderabad, Calcutta and Bhagalpur were sent to Pakistan for arms training through an agent in Calcutta. The agent, Shafqat Ali Siddiqui, was smuggling Muslim youth to Pakistan via Bangladesh and was paid by the Pakistanis for the job. The training in Pakistan included handling of AK-47 rifles and light machine guns and manufacture of bombs with RDX.

By the mid-nineties, the ISI extended its targeted sections and roped in dalits (backwards) and Other Backward Classes (OBCs), along with Muslims, and started training them for subversive activities against India. The criminal mafia of Nepal, Mumbai and Dubai were some of the channels which actively helped and funded such dubious organisations, promoting a nexus among Muslims, dalits and OBCs at ISI's bidding.

The ISI tried to target leaders, teachers, and students of such renowned Muslim organisations as Darul-Uloom Deoband, Ahle Hadis, Darul Uloom Nadvatul (Lucknow) and the Tabligh Jamaat. Certain Muslim political parties of India are also vulnerable to ISI's designs because of their financial dependence on pan-Islamic countries.

10 PROFILE OF SOME PAKISTAN-BACKED MILITANT OUTFITS

HIZB-UL-MUJAHIDEEN (HuM)

Date of formation : September 1989

Affiliations : Hizb-e-Islami Afghanistan (Hikmatyar),

Jamaat ul-Islah (Egypt), Rabita Alam Islami (KSA), Jamaat Amal Kharia, Sharjah, World Kashmir Freedom Movement (UK), Kashmir American Council (USA), Jamaat-e-Islami, Pak/POK and Jamaat-e-Islami, Bangladesh. It gets limited cooperation in certain areas of Jammu and Kashmir with HUA, Lashkar-e-Tayyiba etc. It has an overbearing presence in Shoora-e-Jehad, an umbrella militant outfit for effective coordination in actions.

Membership profile : Includes sizable number of foreigners, mainly Pakistanis or Afghanis.

Overground front : J&K Jamaat-e-Islami (JEI)

MUSLIM MUJAHIDEEN (MM)

Formation : January 1993.

Affiliations : Al Mujahid Force, Muslim Conference of POK. Though decimated with the arrest of its top leaders, it has tactical cooperation with other outfits. A sizable section of its cadres joined Tehrik-e-Jehad floated in April 1997 at the instance of Pakistani authorities. It is a splinter group of HuM.

Membership profile	:	Around five to seven per cent mercenaries. Most members from POK or Pakistan.

AL BARQ

Formation	:	February 1990
Affiliations	:	Markaz Dawat-ul-Arshad, Pakistan. Has limited tactical cooperation with other pro-Pakistan outfits like Muslim Mujahideen, Al Jehad Force and IUM in certain areas of Jammu and Kashmir. A significant sections of its cadres joined Tehrik-e-Jehad.
Membership Profile	:	Around 25 per cent mercenaries, mostly Afghans.
Overground Front	:	J & K People's Conference

AL JEHAD FORCE

Formation	:	December 1991
Affiliations	:	Limited tactical cooperation with other militant outfits, including HuA, LET, HuM, TUM. It is a constituent of Shoora-e-Jehad.
Membership profile	:	Has five to ten per cent alien mercenaries and comprises of mostly Pakistani nationals.
Overground Front	:	J & K People's League

HARKAT UL-ANSAR (HUA)

Predominantly an Afghan militant outfit, HUA was formed in October 1993 following the merger of Harkat-ul-Jehad-e-Islami (HUJI-1980) and Harkat ul-Mujahideen (HuM-1985). It is a formidable pan-Islamic terrorist organisation with an overbearing presence of foreign militants. It was banned by the US on October 8, 1997 after which a section of its cadres joined Tehrik-e-Jehad.

Its volunteers have participated in terrorist operations in Myanmar, Tajikistan and Bosnia, apart from Jammu and Kashmir. Majority of HuA terrorists include those who took an active part in Afghan war. They are called as Mehman Mujahideen or Afghanis, though most of them used to be Pakistanis or Kashmiris. But their strict religious and Islamic appearance like long beard and Pathani suits, give the impression of their being Afghanis. HUA militants also include those from Jammu, Doda, Bhadarwa and Kishtwar.

HuA's affiliations are : Jamat-ul-Ulema-e-Islami, Pakistan; Hizb-e-Islami, Somalia; and units in Pakistan, Bangladesh, Tajikistan, apart from Jamaat-Ahle-Hadis, Pakistan. It works under tactical cooperation with Hizb ul-Mujahideen and Al Jehad force in certain areas.

HuA is headed by one Maulana Abu Taib who is assisted by two deputies— Sajjad Khan and Amjad Bilal. Its main office is in Lahore at 192, J-9/9, Sham Nagar Road, Main Burji Chowk. The addresses of other HuA offices are as follows :

In Lahore :

(i) 247, Huma Block, Kali Kothi, Iqbal Town, Lahore. Phone no. 7831036.

(ii) 159-G, Masjid Chowk, Opposite Eddy Centre, Defence Society, Lahore Cantt. Phone no. 893420.

(iii) Lal Masjid, Begumpura, Lahore. Phone no. 6820489.

(iv) House no 1, Gali no 1, Aftab Park, Shezan Factory, Bund Road, Lahore.

In Muzaffarabad :

Daftar Harkat-ul-Ansar, Ali Akbar Awan High School, Upper Chattar, Muzaffarabad. Phone no 4224, Fax no 2002.

HuA is one of the most potent and deadly outfit among all militants operating in Jammu and Kashmir. It has as many as

16,000 personnel, 5,000 of whom are foreign militants. HuA militants are fanatic Sunni Muslims and distinguish from other Sunni Muslims by describing them as Ansar, the term given to actual Muslim residents of Medina by Prophet Mohammed. Besides Sunni Ulema, ASSP (Anjuman Sipah-e-Sahaba, Pakistan) also backs the outfit.

Huji, which is one of the components of Harkat ul-Ansar, had been founded in February 1980. It owed allegiance to Ahmed Shah Masood and fought in the Afghan war under Masood's leadership for nearly 12 years. Harkat ul-Majahideen, which was formed in 1985, owed its allegiance to Maulana Fazlur Rahman, who is also the Amir of Jamiat-ul-Ulema-e-Islam (Fazlur group).

The HuA represents 'Deobandi' school of thoughts (Sunni) similar to those of Jamiat-ulema-Islam of Fazlur Rehman. Fazlur Rehman group has a solid following in NWFP and Baluchistan.

HuA is dominated by HUJI which was formed in February 1980 under the leadership of Amir, Maulana Ershad Ahmed. The Jehadi activities of HUJI began when Ershad Ahmed, Qazi Saifullah Akhtar and Maulana Abdus Samad Siyal went to Afghanistan on February 25, 1980 and fought the war along with Ahmed Shah Masood and Rabbani's forces. On June 25, 1985, Ershad Ahmed alongwith his 15 associates was killed. 47 other Mujahideen including two Commanders, Maulana Zuber Ahmed Khalid and Maulana Abdur Rehman Farooqi were also killed and scores of Mujahideen were injured. Maulana Saifullah Akhtar then succeeded him as Amir. On April 26, 1992 HUJI Mujahideen entered Kabul along with Masood. Till date, HuA is critical of Hikmatyar and his outfit Hizb-e-Islami. Besdies Masood, Afghan leaders Arslan Rehmani and Maulvi Yungas Khalis also patronise HuA.

HuA has imparted military training in the past to Afghans and other Arab/Asian mercenaries in its Afghan-based training centres. It trained the first batch of Myanmar students in 1993, many of whom are still involved in insurgency activities in Arakan. The first group of its militants went to fight in Bosnia in early 1992 and the second in latter half of 1993 to train and fight for local Muslims. HuA Central Amir, Maulana Saadatullah Khan said that HuA had changed the shape of movements in Kashmir, Bosnia, Tajikistan and Myanmar. Its militants were killing Jews, Hindus and communists. They would establish the Khilafat system over the world, including Washington and Moscow by hoisting the flag of Islam. Maulana Fazal-ur-Rehman Khalil, First Naib Amir, HuA said that the slogan "we do not want Kalashnikov" was a blasphemous slogan.

Harkat-ul-Ansar had organised a meeting in Lahore on November 14/15, 1993 to co-ordinate its worldwide terrorist activities. This was attended among others by the representatives from Tajikistan, Palestine, Hizb-e-Islami (Khalis-Afghanistan) and its area commanders from Islamabad, Peshawar, Muzaffarabad, Karachi, Faislabad and Lahore.

In Kashmir, the militant activities of HuA began in 1989 when the first batch of HUJI militants led by Commander Mazaffar Hussain Shah crossed over to the Valley. There, the group recruited over 300 Kashmiris. In 1990, Commander Sajjad Shahid Afghani, R/o Rawalakot (POK) then related to TuM started terrorist operations in Kashmir in the name of Jehad-e-Hind. He was sent to Kashmir by Maulana Mohd. Farooq Kashmiri, the then Central Amir of TuM. Commander Sajjad Shahid Afghani who took training in Afghanistan and participated in many activities there, was arrested by the Indian Army on January 10, 1994 in Srinagar alongwith Maulana Mohd Masud Azhar, r/o Bahawalpur, Punjab, leader of HuA and Chief Editor Sada-e-Mujahid (Islamabad monthly) and Al-Irshad.

In 1991, Amjad Bilal Kashmiri infiltrated into the Valley and established its main terrorist training camp there. So far, thousands of Kashmiris have been given arms and weapons training. HuA is not financially sound and it faces shortage of funds and weapons. However, these militants are expert in hand-to-hand fight and guerrilla warfare.

In Nov. 1992, Nasarullah Mansur Langaryal infiltrated into the Valley. From November 1992 onwards HuA militants activities got momentum. HuA militants numbering about 16,000 include about 5,000 foreign militants with the ratio of 30 per cent against 70 per cent Doda and Ladakh are the regions where HuA is most active. However, it operates in Srinagar, Bandipura, Kupwara, Sopore and Pulwama also.

HuA leaders at a conference on November 9-10, 1994 at Jamila Ashrafia, Lahore, were of the view that Jehad of Kashmir was not a war of accession or autonomy but was for the existence of Muslims and security of Muslims of South Asia. They were unanimous that the UN was an institution for genocide of Muslims. To operate and learn training of arms and weapons was the culture of Muslims. No one could now save India from disintegration. Dr. Ghulam Qadir Wani, patron, Islamic Students League, said that HuA was the last ray of hope for Kashmiri Muslims. Maulana Mohd Farooq Kashmiri, Central Amir HuA, said that the morale of Kashmir militants was high. Maulana Mohd Ilias Dirve, who recently returned from Kashmir said that HuA started hand-to-hand fight in Kashmir.

In Feb 1995 HUA installed jehad camps at Dubar Chowk, Allama Iqbal Tona, Chaburje Chowk and many other places in Lahore and distributed literature. Maulana Allah Wasaya Qasim, Central leader addressing a gathering at main jehadi camp at Faisal Chowk, said that Kashmir would be freed through jehad. He said that hundreds of HuA militants were fighting against infidelity in Kashmir today.

HuA is maintaining a current Account No. 2389-88 at Habib Bank, Super Market Branch, Islamabad. Drafts and contributions are sent in favour of Saadat Ullah Khan to this account. The address of the outfit in Islamabad is 192-I-9/4, Islamabad and at Muzaffarabad is PO Box No 53, Muzaffarabad.

Maulana Fazlur Rehman, Dy Chief of HuA and Jamiul Rehman (HuA) came to Saudi Arbia to participate in the 34th

Session of the Muslim World League (MWL) held in Makkah from December 30, 1995 to January 3, 1996. They were invited by WAMY Riyadh as special guests to deliver lecture on the topic 'Situation in Kashmir' in a Seminar organised by WAMY in Riyadh. Khalik delivered a virulent anti-India speech abusing 'Hindus' and accusing Indian Armed forces of extreme excesses in J & K. He revealed that 2000 foreign missionaries were fighting in J&K for jehad. Their visit to Saudia Arabia was an evidence of HuA's links with WAMY and Saudi Arabia.

Command Structure of HuA in Pakistan/POK

1. Maulana Sahadatullah Amir in Pakistan, r/o Karachi, Pakistan.

2. Mohd Masood Azhar, Secretary General, r/o 6-B, 1260/108, Kansar Colony, Model Town, Bhawalpur, Pakistan (Arrested on 11.2.94)

3. Maulana Fazal-ur-Rehman Khalik Naib Amir in Pak and General Secretary JUI, Pakistan. R/o Dera Ismail Khan, Frontier Province, Pak (Incharge Finance, General Administration, Militancy)

4. Maulana Abdul Zabbar Kazami, Naib Amir-e-Ala and Military Advisor.

5. Maulana Farooq Kashmiri, r/o Muzaffarabad, POK, Commander-in-Chief of HuA in POK.

6. Mufti Asghar, Launching Chief of HuA.

Yossef Bodansky has highlighted the importance of militant outfits like Harkat ul-Ansar to Islamabad in his book "Bin Laden —The Man Who Declared War On America". Bodansky discusses how the Benazir Bhutto government gave false assurances to Saudi Arabia on discontinuing it support to Kashmir militants. Following are the relevant extracts :

"On instructions from King Fahd, Prince Turki (bin Faisal), head of the Saudi secret and intelligence services) travelled to

Islamabad in early March (1995) for high-level consultations with Bhutto. The main subject was the nature of cooperation in areas of intelligence and terrorism between Pakistan and Iran. Prince Turki told Bhutto that Riyadh was extremely apprehensive about the Saudi 'Afghans' operating in and out of Pakistan and Afghanistan. Turki stressed that Islamabad was the key to the entire Islamist infrastructure because the 'Afghan' camps in Afghanistan were still under the control of the ISI. Most worrisome was the organisation of operational units for the revival of jihad overseas under the banner of Harkat ul-Ansar, which had, and still has headquarters and schools all over Pakistan and a host of military camps in Afghanistan. Harkat ul-Ansar enjoyed and still enjoys close cooperation with the ISI, at minimum in connection with operations in Indian Kashmir and with the Afghan government.

"Prince Turki offered Bhutto a deal. In addition to generous financial assistance, Riyadh would use its power and influence in Washington to lobby for Pakistan interests if the ISI contained the Saudi 'Afghans'; the Saudis would work for repeal of the Pressler Amendment (which imposed stiff sanctions on Pakistan, including the cessation of all military assistance and deliveries, because of its reckless military nuclear programme), would seek economic and technical assistance for Pakistan, and would oversee a public relations blitz about Islamabad's crackdown on militant Islamists. Aware of the crucial importance of Pakistan-Iranian relations for Islamabad and the importance of the 'Afghan' movement for both Islamabad and Teheran, Prince Turki asked Bhutto just for assurances that the ISI would limit the ability of Saudi 'Afghans' to travel to the Middle East. Bhutto promised to cooperate with Riyadh, and Riyadh provided tremendous support during Bhutto's visit to Washington in early April 1995 and in subsequent negotiations on Capitol Hill. A personal emissary from Prince Turki went to Islamabad several times to consult with senior ISI officials on the promotion of Pakistan's image in the United States, by among other methods, publicising its commitment to fighting Islamist terrorism and drug smuggling.

"From the very beginning, however, Islamabad had no intention of honouring the Saudi requests. As far as the ISI was concerned, the entire effort was aimed at changing Pakistan's image rather than containing the spread of Pakistani-sponsored Islamist terrorism. Just how much for show these arrangements had been was revealed in early April 1995, on the eve of Bhutto's trip to the United States. Under cover of another PAIC conference (Popular Arab and Islamic Conference) in Khartoum, secret consultations to coordinate terrorist activities took place between high-level intelligence officials from the key terrorist-sponsoring states and terrorist leaders.

"In late March and early April 1995, Osama bin Laden attended these meetings in Khartoum... The main subject of discussion was establishing a new series of offices and headquarters all over the world so that the international Islamist movement could better cope with forthcoming challenges."

11 LASHKAR-E-TAYYIBA

The Lashkar-e-Tayyiba (LT) was formed in 1990 in the Afghan Province of Kunar. It is a hard-core armed wing of the Markaz-ul-Daawa-wal-Irshad (MDI). The ISI funds, arms and trains its militants and launches them in Kashmir for Jehad. It has militants from Afghanistan, Sudan, Bahrain, Turkey and other Muslim countries besides Pakistan. The LT reportedly imparts training to 4000 youth annually. At least 1500 LT militants have crossed over to Kashmir since 1991.

Its office bearers are—

1.	Commander Zaki-ur-Rehman r/o Renala Khurd (Punjab)	Founder Amir LT Incharge Markaz-e-Tayyiba Hajji, Kunar, Afghanistan.
2.	Nasar Javed	Amir, Maskar-e-Tayyiba Kunar, Afghanistan.
3.	Ustad Abdul Qadir	Instructor, M. T. Kunar
4.	Shabir	—do—
5.	Maulana Abdur Rehman	—do—

MILITANT RECRUITING CENTRES

There are a number of militant recruiting centres of LT in Pakistan and POK. Some of them are as under :

PAKISTAN

1. Markaz ud Daawa Wal Irshad, Chamberlane Road, Mochi Gate, Lahore,

   Phone : 7231106, FAX : 92-42-7228894

2. Markaz ud Daawa Wal Irshad, Bait-ul-Mujahideen Akbar Street, Academy,

   Town : Peshawar

   Phone : 840646

3. Street No. 29

   House No : 1200, 1—10—9 Islamabad

POK

4. Bait-ul-Majahideen

   Near MP Check Post, Nisar Camp,

   Chelabandi, Muzaffarabad

Lahore, Islamabad and Muzaffarabad Centre are mainly engaged in recruiting militants for Jehad in Kashmir, while Peshawar Centre is responsible for recruitment for Jehad in Afghanistan.

Training Centres

Known training centres of LT in POK, Pakistan and Afghanistan are :

POK

Masker Umm-ul-qura, Muzaffarabad, POK
Kotli
MX 9042
Samana (RD 1596)
Badar near Athmuqam Chelabandi in Muzaffarabad

Pakistan

Lahore

Sialkot

Islamabad

Afghanistan

Maskar-e-Tayyiba, Kunar.

Maskar-e-Aqsa in Kunar province (for conducting special courses).

Funds

LT receives funds from ISI, MDI and from Saudi Arabia. Some other Islamic countries are also believed to be providing financial assistance.

There are following two known funds for Kashmir Jehad :—

(a) Bantat-e-Jehad-e-Kashmir.

(b) Jehad-e-Kashmir and Bosnia Committee.

Each Markaz activist is required to contribute 10 per cent of his monthly income to the Jehad Funds. Contributions are deposited in Markaz's Account No : 2011816001, Faisal Islamic Bank of Behar in, Shahrah-e-Quaid-e-Azan Lahore or sent directly to Markaz, Chamberlane Road Office.

Activities

Lashkar-e-Tayyiba militants are engaged in militant activities in Kashmir along with Tehrik-ul-Mujahideen and Al-Barq militants.

MDI has acknowledged that since September 1991 till November 1996, 193 LT militants, mostly belonging to Pakistan and Afghanistan have been killed in Kashmir. It has also claimed that LT has launched 226 operations in Kashmir and killed 3210 SFS including 6 Colonels, 16 Majors, 17 Captains and 6 others Ranks during this period.

The Markaz Jamiat Ahl-e-Hadith and Tulba-e-Markaz regularly hold Jehad conferences and gathering in the name of Jehad-e-Hadith conference, these gatherings instigate masses, especially youth to take part in militancy in Kashmir.

LT activities were noticed in UK in 1996 also. Some members of the LT were reportedly in contact with Pakistani national Malik Mansoor Ahmad, who recruited some Pakistanis living in Europe and financed them to reach Pakistan. On arrival, these volunteers were taken on the strength of LT and sent to the training camps in POK.

LT militants endeavor to bring "awakening" among the Muslims of India so that they stand and fight unitedly. Their ultimate aim is to create chaos in India and carry on with Jehad.

Nexus between LT and Punjab extremists has also been established.

12 Tehrik-e-Jehad

Tehrik-e-Jehad (TeJ) also called Tehrik-ul-Jehad (TuJ) was floated in early 1997 by the ISI with the cadres drawn from Al Barq, Muslim Mujahideen, Ansar ul-Islam and Muslim Liberation Army, with its headquarters at Lahore. Its office in POK is located at Nissar Camp, Chelabandi near Muzaffarabad. Some retired Pak Army personnel were also inducted into the outfit. The aim and objective of the outfit was to wage armed struggle for annexation and merger of Kashmir with Pakistan. These retired army personnel had been entering the bordering areas to help the intruding militants and returning after few days. The main job of the outfit was to launch militants and smuggle arms and ammunition into J&K. The ISI tried to project this outfit in the Valley but failed because its cadres were not that strong in the Valley.

2. Its strength was around 50-60 at the time of its inception. The following are its office bearers:

(a) Amir	-	Farooq Qureshi (earlier Amir of Al Barq), r/o Srinagar.
(b) Naib Amir	-	Salim Wani (earlier Supreme Commander Ansar-ul-Islam). r/o Sopore.
(c) Central Leader	-	Javed Jehangir

(d)	Military Advisor	-	Major (retd) Tariq is the brain behind the organisation. He is the guiding spirit of the outfit.
(e)	Launching Commander of Chham area		Tariq Zia, r/o Sultan Dakki, Uri.
(f)	Launching Commander, Forward Kahuta	-	Badshah Khan, r/o Bunivar Baramulla
(g)	Launching Commander, Leepa area	-	Shaheen

PART IV

BIN LADEN AND TALIBAN

13 Osama Bin Laden

In early January 1980, a young Arab flew to Pakistan. That was a few days after the Soviet Union had invaded and occupied Afghanistan. His visit was in response to an international appeal for help by Mujahideen who were in a disarray, stunned by an unexpected act of a super power.

The young man, a wealthy civil engineer whose business was booming, found the atmosphere in Pakistan nonchalant. No concrete action was taking shape in this Islamic country even though a neighbouring country had been attacked and occupied by a non-muslim State for the first time since World War II. Pan-Islamism and Arab unity were just empty words.

He found the situation in Afghanistan no better. The Mujahideen had no infrastructure to wage even a semblance of war to drive the Soviets out of Afghanistan. American help was coming covertly but the Mujahideen could hardly cope with the combined raids of the Soviets and the Soviet puppet regime of Afghanistan.

The young Arab was clear in his mind that Afghanistan needed him and decided to stay put there to organise "jihad" against the Soviets. In fact, subsequent developments were to prove that he needed Afghanistan as much as Afghanistan needed him. He was to say in one of his press interviews a couple of years later that Islam offered a special place in life-after-death for those who participated in a jihad and "One day in Afghanistan was like a thousand days of praying in an ordinary mosque."

Osama bin Laden had arrived.

Like ordinary wealthy Arabs, bin Laden, too, was a happy-go-lucky, carefree bird and maintained a flashy lifestyle during his youth. Whenever he got a chance to go out of his puritan native country, Saudi Arabia, and visit the westernised Beirut city during his high school days, he used to visit night clubs. Like other spoilt brats, he used to gamble in casinos and drink away to glory in bars, often getting into brawls. He had a hyperactive libido and was known to be a womaniser, too.

But that was more than a quarter century ago. A turning point came in 1973 when his lifestyle started changing dramatically. He turned towards spirituality when he rebuilt two mosques.

Son of Mohammad bin Laden, an affluent businessman engaged in civil construction works, Osama followed in his father's footsteps —initially— and became a qualified civil engineer. Mohammad bin Laden had migrated to Saudi Arabia from the province of Hadramout in South Central Yemen in early twenties. Osama is one of the fifty children his father had sired from several wives. The computer-literate Osama had studied economics and management in a top school in Jeddah, Saudi Arabia.

He watched his father's business empire expanding quickly during the oil boom of the 1970s. Mohammad bin Laden's company, the Bin Laden Corporation, soon won favours of the ruling royal family of Saudi Arabia and secured many big government contracts. By mid-seventies, the Bin Laden Corporation had established itself as one of the top construction companies of Saudi Arabia and had expanded business in many Middle Eastern countries.

The most important turning point in Osama bin Laden's life came when the Soviets invaded Afghanisan in the last days of 1979. His life underwent a sea change as he jumped into the Afghan war cauldron and emerged as a hero of the Islamic world. There has been no looking back for him since then.

The United States turned a blind eye towards his exploits in Afghanistan, little realising that the same revolutionary fury of bin Laden would one day be directed against Washington.

For the United States today, bin Laden is the "Most Wanted Terrorist" on whose head Washington has kept a reward of five million US dollars. Probably never before in the history of terrorism, a super power has launched missile attacks in foreign countries as the US did in case of bin Laden in August 1998.

Though the US fired as many as sixty Cruise missiles on bin Laden's suspected hideouts in Afghanistan and Sudan, the targetted man remained elusive. The Americans came very close to tracking him down last year when they picked up his movement in Afghanistan as the fugitive's whereabouts were revealed by his satellite phone. But bin Laden proved to be one step ahead of the Americans here also and got away after switching off his satellite phone. Since then, probably he has not used his satellite phone.

When bin Laden reached Afghanistan, he was a family man who had established himself as a civil engineer of repute. He had the reputation of building any types of bunkers in any terrain and he demonstrated his expertise soon. He gave up his palatial, airconditioned house in Saudi Arabia to dig trenches in Afghanistan and live in them. He continues to lead a spartan life with his four wives —two Saudi, one Syrian-Palestinian and one Philipino - and some fifteen children. Two of his teenaged sons, Omar and Saad, are also in exile with him in Afghanistan since 1996.

Bin Laden, a graduate from King Abdul Aziz University in Jeddah, addressed himself to two immediate tasks in Afghanistan. First, to recruit as many volunteers as possible to take on the Soviets. The second task was much tougher : preparing a war infrastructure in Afghanistan, a country to which he did not belong.

Starting from scratch, bin Laden raised an organisational structure for recruiting volunteers to fight for Islam against the Soviets. He set up the Maktab al-Khidamat (the Mujahideen

Services Bureau) for overseeing the recruitment work. Thousands of Mujahideen were eventually recruited by bin Laden in a couple of years. The first few batches of Mujahideen were brought to Afghanistan from different Islamic countries by bin Laden at his personal expense. His recruitment centres were spread across 50-odd countries, including the United States and United Kingdom.

Proving that he was an excellent organiser, bin Laden's Mujahideen Services Bureau did not induct just fighters. Doctors, engineers, drug pushers and even terrorists were also brought to Afghanistan, each category having a specialist role. He simultaneously helped establish a drug trafficking network also to finance the ongoing'jihad'.

Simultaneously, he turned his attention to building fortifications to protect Mujahideen from the Soviet artillery. Bin Laden holds a degree in civil engineering as well as a graduate degree in Economics, obtained in 1979. One of the first tasks he undertook was bringing some of the family's bulldozers to Afghanistan. He personally supervised construction of roads to transport heavy equipment which he was to get delivered from some Middle Eastern countries, including Saudi Arabia, shortly later.

Bin Laden also constructed tunnels. These tunnels would open up near Soviet encampments and Mujahideen would come out and surprise the Soviets.

The importance of these fortifications was not lost on the Soviet Union and its puppet Afghan regime and soon their combined forces started launching air raids on the Mujahideen engaged in beefing up their defences. But bin Laden led the Mujahideen from the front and continued with his construction activities, risking his personal safety.

Afghanistan was thus ready with a basic war infrastructure of bunkers, trenches, roads, storage depots, tunnels and even hospitals. Bin Laden and his band of Mujahideen worked round the clock, many times in the face of Soviet fire.

Bin Laden always liked to work on several fronts simultaneously. He constantly kept shuttling between Pakistan and Afghanistan. In the meanwhile, he was also busy with setting up camps in Pakistan and Afghanistan for training of the Mujahideen. A host of Arab terrorist groups soon started using Peshawar as a nerve center of their operations. By 1985, Afghanistan was swarming with Islamic militants from all over the world and an umbrella body, "International Jihad Organisation" was formed to coordinate among these outfits.

After having created the war infrastructure and organising a steady flow of the Mujahideen, bin Laden switched over to the next job he had not done so far : fighting along side the Mujahideen, he took to the battlefield as fish takes to water.

By now, bin Laden had developed connections with fundamentalist elements in Egypt and Algeria. He was used by Saudi authorities to promote political dissidence in Yemen. He used these contacts and his family's wealth to set up his own empire of several companies and banks in Saudi Arabia and Sudan. In 1985, he also formed the Islamic Salvation Fund (Al Qaida), which was actively supported by functionaries of the Egyptian Al Jehad.

In 1986, another turning point came in bin Laden's life. He moved into Eastern Afghanistan (Nangarhar) to take part in fighting against the Soviet forces there. By now he was involved in the fighting operations also, under the Hizb-e-Islami of Gulbuddin Hekmatiyar. One of his major scenes of action was the battle of Jalalabad.

Bin Laden serviced Hekmatiyar's "Al Badr" training camps in Khost, paying salary to instructors at the rate of 3500 to 4000 US dollars per month. About 700 Afghans and Arabs were trained at these camps, alongwith a few thousand Pakistanis and Kashmiris from POK and Jammu and Kashmir.

A Palestinian Mujahideen, Hamza Muhammad, who fought with bin Laden in Afghanistan, brought out the leadership qualities of bin Laden in an interview with a western news agency as follows : "He was a hero to us because he was always on the front line, always moving ahead of everyone else. He not only gave his money, but he also gave himself. He came down from his palace to live with the Afghan peasants and the Arab fighters. He cooked with them, ate with them, dug trenches with them. That was bin Laden's way."

Bin Laden is believed to have moved his residence from Saudi Arabia to Khartoum, Sudan, in 1991. This was the time when his relations with the Saudi rulers started souring as he did not approve of their pro-US policies.

He opened a bank account in the Al Shamall Islamic Bank, Khartoum with investments of over 50 million US dollars. He established several financial companies in Sudan — Wadi al Aqiq Company Ltd, dealing in exports-imports; Toba Investment Company Ltd, dealing in agricultural exports, covering gum, corn, sunflower and sesame projects; and Al Hijrah Construction and Development Ltd. He also established a trading company in Kenya and a ceramic manufacturing company in Yemen.

Some of these ventures were suspected to be fronts for channeling funds to Islamic militants in the Middle East, Africa, UK and USA. Bin Laden developed a special relationship with the Sudanese powerful leader, Hassan al Turabi and Tunisian leader, Rashid al Ghanouchi.

During his sojourn in Sudan, bin Laden revolutionised the infrastructure of that country by constructing airports, highways, dams and military installations worth billions of dollars, much to the consternation of the US.

By mid-1990s, he had forged very close ties with the Iraqi intelligence. So close that Iraq President Saddam Hussain sent a diplomat, Faruq-al-Hijazi, as his personal envoy to meet bin Laden in Kandahar. As a goodwill gesture, Saddam Hussein's envoy handed bin Laden an invaluable gift which would ensure him safe international travel : a pack of blank genuine Yemeni diplomatic passports. These travel documents were given to the Iraqi intelligence by the Yemen intelligence.

By early 1994, bin Laden was proving to be an acute embarrassment to Saudi Arabia. He was going full steam to create a formidable network of Islamic fundamentalists all over the world in such countries as Sudan, Somalia, Iraq, Iran, Egypt, Yemen, Turkey and several western countries, apart from Saudi Arabia itself.

Bin Laden had already come in close contact with such leading Islamic fundamentalists as Sheikh Omar Abdul Rahman of the Egyptian Al Gama Al Islamiya, Sheikh Abdullah Azam (the Arabic cleric who was later murdered in Peshawar, possibly by the ISI), Ayman Al Zawahiri, the Egyptian terrorist belonging to Islamic Al Jehad and Saudi dissident and Al Mashari of the Council for Defence of Legitimate Rights (CDLR) of the UK.

In February 1994, under increasing US pressure, Riyadh revoked bin Laden's Saudi nationality for acts against the State which were construed not in line with the official view of the regime.

Bin Laden's involvement was suspected in the following terrorist actions :

* Providing safe house in Pakistan to World Trade Centre bombing suspect — Ramzi Ahmed Yousef.
* Attack on US soldiers in Yemen and Somalia during peace-keeping operations in 1993.
* Bombing of Khobar Towers, Dhahran, in 1996 in which 19 US Servicemen were killed.
* Somalia's daring, well-planned attempt to assassinate Egyptian President Hosni Mubarak in 1995.
* Bombing of US embassies in Kenya and Tanzania in August 1998. Mohd Sadiq Howaida, an arrested aide of Bin Laden, confessed to Bin Laden's involvement.

In February 1998, bin Laden formed an International Islamic Front (IIF) for 'jihad' against jews and crusaders and named as his deputy, Mustafa Hamza, an Egyptian close associate of Zawahiri. Fazlul al Rahman, a top leader of Pakistan's Harkat ul-Ansar is known to have been deeply involved with this organisation, thus proving bin Laden's involvement in terrorism in Kashmir.

In July 1998, Sheikh Rafai Ahmed Taha, leader of Egyptian Al Gama Al Islamia (Agai) disassociated himself from the IIF.

Intelligence reports indicate that bin Laden's above-named aides — Abdul Aziz Al Masir, Abu Haser, Abu Hazir and Aby Ibrahim have at different times used India as a transit point. In April 1997, for example, one Abdul Salam, a Yemeni, visited Kandahar via Amritsar, using Ariana Afghan Airlines, ostensibly to meet bin Laden.

In April 1998, there were reports of an attempt by a US commandos team to capture bin Laden. The American commandos had entered Afghanistan from Peshawar and proceeded surreptitiously towards Kandahar. The plan did not work as some former Khad agents, now in Taliban's payrolls, betrayed.

Soon afterwards, bin Laden shifted his base from Kandahar to Fahimhaddah, near Jalalabad. His whereabouts have remained unknown, particularly since the US missile attacks in August 1998.

In February 1999, bin Laden was reported to have disappeared from his hideout in Kandahar along with some of his supporters. Initial reports said his family was still in Kandahar, Pakistani media said bin Laden was sighted in Nimroz. An Arab daily, Al Hayat, reported that he had moved towards Baghlan, the area controlled by Hizb-e-Islami (H) pro-Taliban Commander, Bashir Baghlani.

Then there was another report which said the bin Laden was shuttling between four bases, two of which were in Kandahar, one in Farahand, one in Uruzgan. On February 23, an Arab daily claimed that bin Laden was in Jalalabad where a Taliban delegation met him. This was denied by Taliban. On June 21, for the first time since bin Laden went underground in February, Taliban spokesman, Mullah Abdul Hai Muttamain, admitted that he was still in Afghanistan but his whereabouts were not known.

An intelligence report said in July 1999 that bin Laden may have shifted his hideout to a newly-constructed location in the vicinity of Bola Boluk, a hilltop in Farah province, off the road from Farah to Daulatabad. Constructions in this area are duly camouflaged and guarded by armed personnel.

Bin Laden, the reports say, travels in this region in a 50-Viper car which is fitted with sophisticated weapons. For security reasons, several of his bodyguards travel in similar cars, masquerading as bin Laden.

US President Bill Clinton signed an executive order on July 6, 1999, imposing economic sanctions on Taliban for harbouring bin Laden. Reacting to this, the Taliban spokesman said Taliban was unaware of bin Laden's movements, though he admitted that the wanted fugitive was in Afghanistan.

In November 1998, bin Laden was invited to attend an Islamist conference in Pakistan. But he dropped his plan to attend the meet as Islamabad discreetly asked him that his proposed visit would cast a shadow over Prime Minister Nawaz Sharif's forthcoming visit to Washington. Bin Laden sent his brief speech to the organisers in which he stressed the need for continuing 'jihad' against Christians and Jews.

"...It is obligatory for all Muslims to continue jihad by sacrificing their wealth and life as long as their holy places are not liberated from the subjugations of Jews and Christians. This freedom is not possible until we sacrifice all our wealth and our lives. As it is a religious obligation for every Muslim to support the Mujahideen fighting for freedom of sacred places, similarly they are also obligated by their religion to support the Taliban government in Afghanistan, because by enforcing Sharia in Afghanistan, Taliban have established the system of God on God's land," bin Laden said in his speech which was read out at the Islamabad conference.

In fact, his unflinching dedication to Taliban and Taliban's refusal to hand over bin Laden to the US even in the face of missile attacks and economic sanctions have given rise to an assessment in the West that bin Laden is actually the chief of Taliban. There are also unconfirmed reports that bin Laden's daughter is married to Taliban leader, Mullah Omar.

Bin Laden's links with Kashmiri militants are well established. There are intelligence reports that Pakistan's Kargil misadventure was also closely worked out between the ISI and bin Laden. There were also "reliable" reports of bin Laden's presence in the POK during the Kargil conflict.

Yossef Bodansky recounts an interesting episode in his book "Bin Laden : The Man Who Declared War on America". Bodansky's account, given below, also drops enough hints which explode the myth that the ISI was not involved in the Kargil conflict :

"By early December, Osama bin Laden had already ackowledged that he was ready for the escalation of his jihad... At this time, an Iraqi intelligence official held a series of meetings in the Iraqi Embassy in Islamabad with the leaders of several Pakistani militant Islamist movements and representatives of the Taliban. These meetings took place with the full knowledge and endorsement of the ISI.

"In the first half of December, bin Laden and Zawahiri arrived in Peshawar, Pakistan, to chair a periodic meeting of the Arab 'Afghan' leaders residing in Pakistan. About a dozen people participated, including Asadallah Abdul Rahman, the son of Sheikh Omar Abdul Rahman of World Trade Centre fame, who was seated next to Zawahiri, symbolising the enduring importance of Sheikh Omar.

"Bin Laden's visit was not a clandestine surge into Pakistan. He was the guest of North West Frontier Province senior officials, including relatives of his fourth wife, and as before during his frequent visits, Pakistani security authorities provided him with a special escort. Bin Laden's other recent visits had been kept quiet, but the Pakistani Islamists highlighted the early December visit as proof of the cooperation they enjoy with Sharif's

Islamabad. As for official Islamabad, the NWFP authorities 'appeared to be ignorant about the reported presence of Saudi dissident, wanted by (the) USA, Osama bin Laden in Pakistan', when they were contacted by a correspondent from *Dawn*, a Pakistani newspaper."

This conclave of Mujahideen in Pakistan coincided with the Pakistani Army's incursions into Kargil in the guise of Mujahideen.

Bin Laden's contacts with Kashmir terrorists are about a decade old. A Palestinian, Abu Mahmood, was suspected to be an intermediary between bin Laden and Al Faran group of Harkat ul-Ansar militants who kidnapped four Western tourists in Jammu and Kashmir in 1995.

One Asadullah, a Muslim of Indian origin residing in Peshawar, is believed to be his contact man for coordinating activities in Jammu and Kashmir. Some Afghan militants and other infiltrators from POK and Pakistan, who were arrested or killed in security operations in Jammu and Kashmir, have been found carrying posters and pamphlets of bin Laden and his statements on Islamic jihad.

The bin Laden menace has assumed even more importance for India now that he has openly declared a 'jihad' against India. On September 17, 1999, a news agency report from Islamabad quoted bin Laden as saying, "Our biggest enemies are the US and India and we should target them using the best of our efforts."

14 TALIBAN

In 1988 there were 1,320 madarsas (Islamic religious schools) in Pakistan Punjab ; in 1995 they swelled to 1,686 and in 1997 to 2,512. Nearly 2,19,000 students are studying in these institutions. They are called "talib-e-ilm" (seeker of knowledge). These people are called "taliban" (plural of "talib") in Afghanistan and the Pashto-speaking areas of Pakistan.

At least 65 per cent of these institutions are run on private funds which come from pious Muslims or foreign donors, many of whom are supporting violent revivalist movements. But that is hardly causing concern to Pakistan government.

The 'madarsas'-educated people of Pakistan and Afghanistan are aware that the ruling elite is corrupt, or widely believed to be corrupt, and has alienated the poor. The angry poor flock to the 'madarsas' because after all, the 'madarsas' give them food and shelter — something which the State does not do. The products of these 'madarsas' reason that the leadership is rightly theirs — votes or no votes. Because, they are the rightful interpreters of the Divine Law. So, they take to the gun to seize power and enforce the Divine Law. This is the 'taliban' rationale.

Pakistani commentator, Tariq Rahman, summed up the Taliban psyche when he wrote in the May 26, 1997 edition of "The News" thus : "Having a medieval mind, loaded with texts which are memorised, their analysis of the world predisposes them to label the enemy as heretical : the whole world is heretical (for the Takfiris); the Shias are heretics (for the Sipah-i-Sahaba), and the list goes on. These people divide society in terms of faith, or assumptions about the other persons' faith. The next logical step for them is either to eliminate the 'other' or convert him/her."

Taliban militia, which by mid-1999 was in control of 90 per cent of Afghanistan, is Pakistan's latest horse in Islamabad's fanatical efforts to control this landlocked country of immense geo-politico-strategic importance.

Central Asia that comprises Afghanistan and five of former Soviet republics — Tajikistan, Kyrgystan, Turkmenistan, Kazakhstan and Uzbekistan— holds significance to the world community mainly due to it being part of the Caspian Sea region. That region has attracted another great energy rush after the Middle East. Afghanistan is a part of this latest 'great game' for oil and gas. Pakistan's Afghan policy is driven by its desire to participate in that game in an effective manner. That game is making strange bedfellows. Iran, Armenia, Russia, Tajikistan, Kazakhstan, Uzbekistan and Kyrgystan, apart from India, are important players in this game. Turkey, though historically suspicious of Russia and currently not on rather friendly terms with Iran, is increasingly being driven to this regional quest for control of potential oil and gas reserves.

China is another very significant player in this game and has immense stakes here which it would not give up easily. The US, too, has huge strategic interests in the region. In fact, China is being viewed as a rival by the Western companies both as investor and as a market.

Pakistan's quest for control of Afghanistan's road system became a major obsession and focal point of ISI's major covert operations by the early nineties — second only to Islamabad's fixation with Kashmir. In 1991, the ISI embarked on a grand plan to control the strategic Kushka-Herat-Kandahar-Quetta highway. This highway, which stretches from former Soviet Central Asia through western and southern Afghanistan, feeds into the road system of southern Pakistan and goes upto Karachi, Pakistan's main port.

The Pakistani strategists realise that this is the only strategic artery which is in good condition and can be rebuilt or repaired to carry long convoys, cutting hugely on time and costs of travel. A network of pipelines along this highway to transfer oil and gas from Central Asia and northern Afghanistan holds the key to Pakistan's future economic development.

With this objective in mind, Pakistan undertook massive repairs of the most damaged sectors of this highway inside Afghanistan. which still continues to be Afghanistan's sole gateway to Western goods. To protect the convoys, the ISI sought to use local Afghan leaders and chieftains. The ISI lured them with money, weapons and outlets for their illicit narcotics they grew in the Helmand Valley in southwestern Afghanistan.

This move created chaos. The local chieftains got involved in bloody battles over the allurements offered by the ISI for ensuring safe passage of the convoys. By 1994, Pakistan found itself confronting a situation wherein most of the ISI-propped chieftains were killed. A new generation of aspiring warlords mushroomed quickly, waiting for the ISI patronage. They got it, but this move, too, backfired. Within months, these greedy guards of the convoys started raiding the convoys they were paid for protecting.

The developments set the ISI bosses thinking. Some way had to be found to achieve total control of this highway. They prepared and put into action a new plan. A new force had emerged on the scene.

The Taliban was born.

It was literally a dream come true for Maulavi Mohammad Omar, who was to become founder Chief of Taliban.

A fiercely devout Muslim from Kandahar, Omar's rise to stardom was phenomenal. Taliban soldiers narrate an interesting story of the modest birth and rise of Taliban. Omar, a veteran Pushtun Mujahideen commander, who turned into a religious student, saw a dream sometime in 1994. The legend has it that Prophet Mohammad came to Omar in the dream and instructed him to put an end to the reign of terror unleashed by his own tribesman who was appointed as a local commander by the ISI. Because of his clout with the ISI, this warlord had become power-drunk and had been raping women and looting the properties of the local Afghanis at will.

Omar got cracking and organised an armed force of fifty former Mujahideen who had served under him in the fight against Soviet forces more than a decade ago. The erring warlord was assassinated by Omar's force and his property and arsenal was seized.

Omar laid down strict rules of conduct. His first task was to distribute the assassinated warlord's riches and property among the needy of Kandahar. With this act, Omar immediately acquired a Robinhood image. And his outfit, the Taliban— students of religious schools— endeared himself to the masses.

Quickly, Omar's base started expanding and hundreds of Mujahideen joined the Taliban. Kandahar was the launching pad for Taliban and the Talban soldiers lost no time in seizing their birth city. The Kandahar seizure in November 1994 was only the beginning of the Taliban campaign.

Both Omar and the ISI were aware of their strategic value to each other. It did not take long for the ISI bosses to realise the importance of Omar and his Taliban. By December 1994, the ISI-Taliban nexus had been forged, much to the consternation of the then ISI protege, Gulbuddin Hekmatiyar.

In the next few years, Hekmatiyar kept complaining to Pakistan against Islamabad's propping up of Taliban and Islamabad kept denying it.

The ISI, in fact, was playing a double game. While arming and supporting the Taliban not-so-secretly, the ISI kept the Hekmatiyar faction in good humour. By December 1994, the ISI had started arming the Taliban with Kalashnikov assault rifles and extending massive logistical support and training to the Taliban.

As the clout of Taliban was increasing phenomenally, its numerical strength, too, was shooting up. The probable scenario of conquering Afghanistan by proxy and making Afghanistan the fifth Province of Pakistan made the Pakistani military strategists drool each time they visualised this scenario.

The migration from Baluchistani 'madarsas' to the Taliban was significant and ought to have rung the alarm bells in the ISI. The ISI had deliberately set up a large number of Sunni 'madarsas' to alter the demographic character of Baluchistan, known for its fiercely independent Baluchi tribes which had time and again raised the banner of revolt against the Federal Government.

But the ISI masters allowed the events unfold themselves and watched with silent appreciation as nearly four thousand youths from 'madarsas' in Baluchistan on Pakistan-Afghanistan border left the 'madarsas' and crossed the border to join Taliban. This was in the middle of December in 1994.

The 1994 end trickle of 'madarsa' products joining the Taliban became a torrent as 1995 dawned. The majority of the migratory birds flying into the Taliban nest were from Baluchistan.

As a result, by February 1995, the Taliban had become a virtual army, its strength having swelled to a fearsome 25,000. It remained a predominantly Pushtun force, though a 1000-odd Ujbeks and Tajiks were also on its rolls.

Within days of its beefed up strength, the Taliban was knocking at the gates of Kabul. The Taliban reached upto Maidan Shahr, some 30 kms south of Kabul, and marched menacingly to Chahar-Siyab, forcing ISI's discarded love, Hekmatiyar, to flee Chahar-Siyab.

While fleeing, Hekmatiyar's men left huge quantities of arms and ammunition which were put to good use by the Taliban in their forthcoming battles against Hekmatiyar.

By the middle of 1995, the Pakistani dream corridor between the Indian Ocean and Central Asia had come in total control of the Taliban.

As the year 1995 rang out, it was clear who was in control of Afghanistan and with whose support. But by now, Pakistan was beginning to feel the pinch of the diplomatic fallout of the Taliban Frankestein it had helped create.

Pakistan's relations with Iran and the neighbouring Central Asian states like Ujbekistan, Tajikistan and Kyrgystan, apart from Russia and Turkey took a nosedive. A major flashpoint came in mid-1998 when the Taliban overran Mazar-i-Sharif, the nerve centre of northern Afghanistan, which is just 60 kms south of the Uzbek town of Termez.

As the Taliban reached the Uzbekistan borders, Uzbek President, Islam Karimov, expressed his apprehension that after having captured total control over Afghanistan, the Taliban would take measures to spread its ideology onto other states, primarily of the Central Asian region. Karimov stressed the need for the five permanent members of the United Nations' Security Council — US, Russia, Britain, China and France—to send their representatives to visit Afghanistan to have a first-hand account of the goings on in Afghanistan.

Russian and Tajik troops were put on high alert along the Tajik border and Moscow warned Islamabad that its continued assistance to Taliban was a threat to international peace and security.

Relations between Pakistan and Iran plummeted as the conquerors of Mazar-i-Sharif killed ten captive Iranian diplomats and an Iranian journalist. Iran has been a fierce opponent of Taliban and continues to support the regime of former Afghan President Burhanuddin Rabbani, who was ousted by the Taliban in 1996.

Iran was also a supporter of the Uzbek warlord, Abdul Rashid Dostum. The fall of Mazar-i-Sharif had caught Iran by surprise.

By the first week of September, 1998, Iran had made a massive build-up along the Afghanistan border as part of its "Ashura 3" exercise.

Iran had deployed as many as 200,000 of its troops along its northeastern border with Afghanistan as 25,000 of the Afghans stood by on the other side to receive them eagerly. Besides, 25 attack aircraft, 80 T-72 tanks, two SA-6 mobile missile batteries, 90 heavy artillery pieces and 60 armoured vehicles were also deployed.

US defence intelligence believed Iran's intentions could be to launch airstrikes and limited ground incursions in Afghanistan to take on Taliban targets. In addition to the military equipment and personnel from the Islamic Revolution's Guard Corps, the Iranians had constructed a 100-bed field hospital, which included a surgery unit and a blood bank facility.

All this led intelligence analysts to conclude that the Iranian exercise was a smoke screen for an incursion into Afghnaistan which was bound to give rise to a full-scale Iran-Taliban war. There were high degree of chances that Pakistan may be sucked into this war. The Shia-dominated Iran was pained with the large-scale massacres of Shias in Mazar-i-Sharif at the hands of the Taliban, an out-and-out Sunni force and was all too eager to even up with the Taliban. But the situation did not deteriorate any further and the feared conflict did not take place.

The Iran-Taliban faceoff, however, cast a shadow over relations between Teheran and Islamabad. Iran squarely held Pakistan responsible for the killings of its diplomats in Afghanistan. "The responsibility for their martyrdom rests on the Taliban militia and the government of Pakistan which had assured us of their safety," the Iranian foreign ministry said in a statement on September 10, 1998.

The Pakistani strategists are not bothered that their nexus with Taliban is going to have serious repercussions on Islamabad. Pakistan's only visible, concrete and expected gains in this whole game were the plans of a pipeline from Turkmenistan to Pakistan via Afghanistan. Just when Taliban was poised to take over the whole of Afghanistan, UNOCAL, the American company which was leading the international consortium constructing that pipeline, announced the suspension of its plans to construct the much trumpeted pipeline.

There are two schools of thoughts in Pakistan over the Taliban. One is euphoric over the Taliban success and treats it as a victory for Pakistani diplomacy. Pakistan's influence, it is believed, will now be predominant in Afghanistan — seen to be a key country from the viewpoint of doing business with Central Asia. The argument goes that the Taliban victory in Afghanistan is a geostrategic victory for Pakistan which will make Islamabad much stronger and influential.

The other school has castigated Pakistan for its involvement in Afghanistan and felt that Pakistan's hosting of the seven Mujahideen parties and its involvement in the war in Afghanistan was a mistake. One powerful argument for this is that Afghanistan is the place where foreigners have always stumbled and made mistakes. The Afghans have never liked foreigners exercising power over them.

Afghanis have taught a lesson to three major superpowers of the day and they had to rue their meddling in Afghan affairs. Britain burnt its fingers twice and made a peace that stopped short of total victory for the Afghans.

The Soviet Union folly in invading and occupying Afghanistan is well known. In fact, many think that the demise of the Soviet Union came a little earlier than expected because of its Afghanistan misadventure.

All regional powers and Pakistan's neighbours have been apprehensive of the Pakistan-Taliban nexus. Former Soviet republics in Central Asia, particularly, are scared of similar revivalist Islamic movements in their countries. They would very much like to see such movements suppressed and the Taliban somehow defeated in Afghanistan. Faced with a Taliban-backed fundamentalist thrust, they are now looking towards Russia for support. And the Russians are willing to stand by them.

The Chinese stand on Taliban cannot be ignored on the Asian chessboard. Though China has signed a couple of agreements with the Taliban, it is bound to be wary of Taliban.

On the one hand, the Chinese are improving their relations with Russia and with as many of former Soviet republics as possible with special reference to the Muslim Central Asian republics and on the other hand, the US is actively wooing China.

China has reasons to look at outfits like Taliban with suspicion because of large muslim population in its strategic Xinjiang (meaning New Territory) province. China's Lop Nor nuclear testing site is located in this province which is believed to have substantial, though as yet untapped oil reserves.

The local Uighur population has a host of reasons to be disenchanted with Beijing. China's attempts to change the demographic character of the province, its strict ban on receipt of funds from abroad for religious purposes, prohibition of religious books not published and printed by the State and a ban on government servants attending prayers in mosques are only some of these irritants.

Beijing is well aware that the most important threat it faces today is from within and the disgruntled Muslims are potential trouble-makers. This was clearly manifested during the three-day-long riots that broke out at Yining near the Kazakh border on February 4, 1997. The official death toll in these riots was nine Uighurs killed, but the Uighur political exiles put the figure at more than 100 Uighurs and at least 25 Han Chinese killed. Besides, at least 31 other Uighurs were executed after their summary trials found them guilty of inciting trouble.

And China must be aware that this may well be just the beginning of a deeper unrest in Xinjiang. Beijing knows that the Uighurs cannot be under-estimated. Between 1944 and 1950, the Uighurs had managed to declare an independent East Turkistan ith the capital Yining. The People's Liberation Army of China ad re-established control over the Chinese mainland in this gion. Some of the Uighur nationalists had crossed over into the ilgit and Baltistan areas of POK from where they went to Saudi rabia and Turkey.

During the Afghan war in the 1980s, Gulbuddin Hekmatiyar ad recruited Sunni Muslims from Xinjiang with China turning e Nelson's eye to the development because it suited its interests. he Chinese Muslims fighting Soviet troops on foreign soil suited eijing both ways, whether the Uighurs survived or died in the attle. But many Uighurs survived and when they returned after ning their skills in Afghanistan, they turned their guns to the an Chinese.

After the Soviet withdrawal from Afghanistan in 1989, oradic incidents of violence took place in Xinjiang. The ovement for an independent state of East Turkistan was revived a big way since the February 1997 riots in Xinjiang.

The China-Pakistan-Taliban-Muslim fundamentalists tangle as important security ramifications for the entire Asian region ad is illustrative of the growing Muslim fundamentalism across e world. In August 1997, the authorities of Xinjiang province iveiled a plan of fencing the border with Pakistan to prevent ans-border activities of fundamentalists and drug pushers. This ove came just about three months after the Pakistan government anded over to China 12 Uighurs wanted in connection with omb explosions in Xinjiang. The wanted Uighurs had infiltrated to the Gilgit area and enrolled themselves in the 'madarsas' ere.

The incident was a flashpoint in Sino-Pakistan relations. B aman, a former Additional Secretary in the Cabinet Secretariat d known for his incisive analyses as Director of the Chennai-sed Institute for Topical Studies, wrote as follows in the IDR sue of April-June 1999 :

"Following the arrest of 16 Pakistan-trained Uighurs i Xinjiang, the Chinese authorities protested to the Pakistan Interic Ministry on January 6, 1999, over this. The Chinese complaine that the arrested persons admitted during their interrogation th: they had been trained in guerilla warfare in training camps : Jalalabad in Afghanistan and at Landi Kotal, in the Khyber Agenc of Pakistan. The Pakistani authorities denied the existence of an training camps for Uighur separatists in Pakistani territory...

"In a surprise move, a five-member Chinese delegation le by Sun Guoxian, head of the Asia desk in the Chinese Foreig Office, visited Kabul in the last week of January, 1999 for tall with officials of the Foreign Ministry of the Taliban governmen Since China has not established diplomatic relations with tl Taliban administration, this visit has been interpreted by many a an indication of a Chinese anxiety to befriend the Taliban i order to dissuade it from helping the Uighurs.

"While this is possible, it is also likely that the Chines action was a quid pro quo gesture in return for the Taliban action in October-November, 1998 in allowing two teams c Chinese ballistic missile experts to examine the places i Afghanistan struck by US Cruise missiles in August last year an take collected samples of the debris to China for furthe examination. The Taliban was also reported to have given to tl Chinese missile experts one of the Cruise missiles which had n exploded."

China has been forced to recognise the threat posed by tl Muslim fundamentalists. A clear indication of this was whe Beijing signed an agreement with Pakistan in March 1995 c upgrading the Karakoram highway to facilitate transit trade, b went slow on the project in view of the spurt in the fundamentali activities.

The highly strategic Karakoram Highway was built by tl Pakistani Army engineers in association with the Chinese exper and technicians. It was completed in 15 years and snakes throug some of the toughest terrain of the world. The 804.67 km (5(miles) metalled road has been described as a marvel of civ engineering and even as "The Eighth Wonder of the World". The Highway is a major security concern for India. The Highway starts from Havelian, nearly 100 kms from Islamabad, and winds through Abbotabad, Manshera, Thakot, Besham, Pattan, Sazin, Chilas, Gilgit, and Hunza to the Chinese Frontier across the 4602 metre (!6,100 feet) high Khunjerab Pass.

The Chinese developed cold feet on upgrading the Karakoram Highway because the proposed road was to run across Xinjiang. The Chinese feared that the new route would inevitably lead to massive influx of Muslim fundamentalists into Xinjiang.

Against the backdrop of all this, the crucial question that arises is what is the cost of Taliban victory for Pakistan ? Apart from the diplomatic reversals and straining of ties with several countries, there are various direct and indirect costs for Pakistan because of the Taliban. The hundreds of thousands of Afghan refugees in Pakistan, the by-product of heroin and gun culture, and the economic burden of supporting the Taliban government are only some of the costs which Pakistan has been paying.

M B Naqvi, while writing in the respected Pakistani daily "The Dawn" in the August 15, 1998 issue, brilliantly summed up the situation as follows :

"The crucial issue today is : how does Pakistan take advantage of its supposedly strengthened position ? Now that Pakistan's influence can be said to be considerable, how does it benefit from it in concrete terms ? This is not the 19th century or the early 20th century. Pakistan is not economically strong enough to become something of a colonial power. It does not have enough capital to invest regionally and reap profits thereafter. Its diplomatic reach and potential are nowhere round even minimally matching those of the US or even of countries like China and India... "There is yet another matter of serious concern : the government in Afghanistan would be short of cash as well as supplies for the population it controls. These supplies have necessarily to go forth from Pakistan even if the Taliban can go and acquire hard currencies to pay for these. It is doubtful if

Pakistan economy can go on bearing such a burden. The financial and economic costs of a patron's role in Afghanistan would be prohibitive for Pakistan."

Another Pakistani commentator, Eqbal Ahmad, writing in "The Dawn" of August 23, 1998, echoed similar sentiments : "Afghanistan's reconstruction cost is conservatively estimated at some $ 40 billion. We cannot muster such amounts even for ourselves, so who will keep the Taliban in business ? The strategic dreamers of Islamabad dream of dollar laden Saudi princes, Emirate Sheikhs and American oil tycoons laying transnational pipelines from Turkmenistan to Karachi. They are veterans of false and deadly dreams such as the great Kashmiri uprising in support of Operation Gibraltar in 1965, or the powerful reinforcements which the American Seventh Fleet was bringing to Pakistan's army in East Pakistan, now Bangladesh.

"Pakistan is being trapped again in risky illusions, and again the people not the decision makers will pay the price. Without the resources of a great power, Pakistan has entered the game — both nuclear and non-nuclear — that great powers found difficult to sustain... Policy-makers in Islamabad assume that a Taliban-dominated government in Kabul will be permanently friendly towards Pakistan. The notion of 'strategic depth' is founded on this presumption. This is an illusion. The chances are that if they remain in power, the Taliban shall turn on Pakistan, linking their brand of Islamism with a revived movement for Pakhtunistan. I have met some of them and found ethnic nationalism lurking just below their 'Islamic' skin. Old loyalties rarely stand in the way of new temptations. Also, as the threat of local rivals recedes, their resentments against Pakistan government shall rapidly augment as Islamabad will not be in a position to meet their expectations of aid."

Eqbal Ahmad maintained that Taliban presented to the world "a most distorted and uniquely repugnant visage of Islam" which is bound to isolate Pakistan from the civilised societies. "The Taliban's," he writes, "is the most retrograde political movement in the history of Islam. The warlords who proscribe music and sports in Afghanistan, inflict harsh punishments upon men for trimming their beards, flog taxi drivers for carrying women passengers, prevent sick women from being treated by male physicians, banish girls from schools and women from the work place are not returning Afghanistan to its traditional Islamic way of life as the western media reports sanctimoniously...

"To call them 'mediaeval' as did the protestors in Teheran is to insult the age of Hafiz and Sadi, of Rabi'a Basri and Masur al-Hallaj, of Amir Khusrau and Hazrat Nizamuddin. The Taliban are the expression of a modern disease, symptoms of a social cancer which shall destroy Muslim societies if its growth is not arrested and the disease is not eliminated. It is prone to spreading and the Taliban will be the most deadly communicators of this cancer if they remain so organically linked to Pakistan... If we must live with a theocracy next door, it is better to live with an enlightened rather than a barbaric version of it."

PART V

APPENDICES

(1) DIARY OF A PAKISTANI SOLDIER

A personal diary of a NLI Lieutenant, Muhammad Maaz Ullah Khan Sumbal, was recovered from Point 4812 in Batalik sub-sector of Kargil. The handwritten diary shows that Lt Sumbal, a well-educated man with a penchant for writing, started off from Rawalpindi at 1400 hours on the New Year day for Skardu by bus.

The diary reveals that the soldier was feeling so home-sick that the same day he called up home several times from several places. His Unit reached Skardu the next morning at 10 O' clock. By January 13, his Unit had taken positions at Baltoro Sector.

The Pakistani soldiers had television in their encampments and often watched Indian satellite TV channels, like Zee Television. The diary, written in reasonably good English, narrates Lt Sumbal's "terrible experience" of taking bath on the height of 19,000 feet when the mercury had dipped to as low as minus 22 degree celsius.

The diary makes repeated mentions of nonchalant attitude of the Pakistani Army personnel who were entrusted with the task of looking after the logistic requirements of the intruders. An entry on February 5, shows that though the temperature had fallen to minus 30 degree celsius, the weather was clear and still the helicopter did not come with food supplies. Some excerpts from Lt Sumbal's diary are reproduced below :

2 ۱۳ رمضان SATURDAY / 3 ۱۴ رمضان SUNDAY

2 Jan. Reached Skardu at 1000 hrs and reported to the unit (8 NLI). Capt Kheed Shams Khan was Adjt. Also Capt Shehryar, Capt Imran & Capt Sarfraz were there. Maj Raheem & Maj Qazi were CO & 2IC resp. Nice team of offrs.

30 ١١ شوال SATURDAY / 31 ١٢ شوال SUNDAY

31 Jan 99. Heli-msn came consisting of 2x Lama's & 1x MI-17. Sick/cas were evac. New supplies dumped. TV set sent for repair. Bundles of eatables and mail were received. I got 2x ltrs from home, 1x Eid Card from Aapa, 1x ltr/Eid Card from Asif, 1x ltr from Mussarrat Abbas, 1x card from Capt Naveed (31 FF) & 1x diary (this one) from Tariq Mamoo.

6th day at IHEC. I took a bath. Terrible Experience — Taking bath at 19,000 ft, at -22°C.
Capt Dr Salah-ud-din Masood left for Nawaz Camp on his way to Conway Saddle. I will be moving up along Capt Sarwar on 10 Feb, انشاء اللہ

It is my 8th day at IHEC. I felt like going on a walk, so made a round trip of the camp. Helipad & Gun-posn. I got an idea of firing the 12.7 mm HMG. Got permission from Zulu and tested the fire of HMG. Nice experience!

4 ١٦ شوال THURSDAY

It is my 9th day at IHEC. The day is crystal clear & Sunny. Zulu decided to check the Guns. So the clear sunny day was celebrated in the roars & thunders of 105 mm Mtn Guns.

10th day at IHEC. Another clear day although not sunny. Saddle all visible with its igloos appearing like black dots on white surface. Last ni, again the sky was crytal clear. Temp falling to -30°C, as I checked the thermometer in the morning. Today, Heli-msn again didn't come despite clear weather.

15th day at IHEC. After spending two weeks at IHEC, today, we left for Nawaz Camp on our way to Conway Saddle — the final frontier. Started at 1530 hrs, we reached at 1700 hrs. Capt Sarwar ex 38 Mtn is accompanying

۲۲ شوال
THURSDAY 11

30th day in Baltoro Sector. We left for Saddle from Nawaz Camp at 0800 hrs in a bad weather, but, by the grace of Allah, it got clear after we crossed C-5 (Rel Pt). Reached the Saddle Camp at 1500 hrs. Capt Dr Salah-ud-din received us with SMG fire.

7th day at Saddle. Finally the weather was a little calm and Himmat Wali & Party was rel. Iqbal & Party came in. We welcomed them with the fire of 12.7mm HMG.

SUNDAY 21/SATURDAY 20

20 Feb. Weather was clear today, although not Sunny. Heli reportedly went to Shakma so no chance. We went to 'Fwd Saddle'. I took along 'Styre Sniper' and shot at Indian Posn. SSG Nullah was also visible in front.

14th day at Saddle. Early morning we were given Alert by Zarrar HQ regarding some en HelBorne Op. I got the Two 12.7 & the 14.5 ready with ammo on. Tested the Styre & SMG for zeroing. Now let the en come. Capt Dr Sohail is today at Nawaz on his way to rel Capt Dr Salah-ud-Din, will be here tommorrow. I am expecting 15 ltrs. Let's see who all wrote them.

27 SATURDAY/28 SUNDAY

27 Feb 99. 17th day at Saddle. Another crystal clear day. Allah is very kind on his soldiers. I got the magazine opened and enjoyed the fire of 60mm Mortar. I fired 3 rounds myself. No Heli msn. Night is also clear with moon & stars. الحمد لله

28 Feb 99. 18th day at Saddle. Another crystal clear sunny day. الحمد لله. Today Two Heli-msn were conducted. Dr Sohail got his Demand — Pepsi, Bread, Nimko, DryFruit etc. MI-17 was in good hands, Good Droppings. Other than ration, K-II, we got fresh fruit aswell — Oranges. Infact, Zulu had asked Capt Murtaza, at Paiju, to send 'Malta' at Saddle. Just imagine!

March 99

۱۳ ذیقعد TUESDAY 2

20th day at Saddle. Again wind & snow, but not that bad. Hopingly, it will be clear tommorrow morning for us to go down. Oh yes! we are completing 21 days at Saddle tommorrow, and getting down also. انشاء اللہ, Got my luggage packed & fastened the krympons onto my shoes. All set to go, by Allah Almighty's Grace.

4 ۱۵ ذیقعد THURSDAY

Today finally we got down from Saddle. Capt Aftab & Capt Tariq releived myself & Capt Sarwar resp. Although not a very clear weather but we moved anyway. Got down to ~~Saddle~~ IHEC and received by Maj Tariq (Zulu) & Co. What a change! Television is operational alongwith the Dish. But unfortunately Telephone is out of order.

7 Mar 99. Again we couldn't move due to Blizzard & Bad Weather. Instead we saw "Doli Saja Ke Rakhna" on Zee TV at ni.

9 ۹ دسمبر
TUESDAY

56th day in Baltoro Sector. A nice & clear morning & so I left for Shama at 0900 although I couldnt see other offrs as they were sleeping. At about 1100, when we were about to come out of the Nullah, Two Llama's flew overhead to IHEC. They took the cas & our Zulu Maj Tariq back to Skardu. So Maj Tariq is also rel today by Maj Khurshid. We reached Shama at 1600 hrs. A tough walk as there was lot of snow & lot of weight on me.

57th day at Baltoro Sector. Left Shama for Concordia. Again passed by K-2. A clear day. But due to lot of snow, a difficult move. Actually, we are the first party out after recent snow fall. ~~No~~ So we are doing track-beating.

58th day at Baltoro Sector. Left Concordia for Gora-II. Met Dr Javed on the way. Reached Gora-II around 1300 hrs. Decided to go ahead upto Gora-I. So moved on and reached Gora-I at 1700 hrs. Received by Dr. Wasif, Capt Faisal, Capt Mudassar.

59th day in Baltoro. Stayed at Gora-I and had a rest. Talked home through wrls.

71st day in Baltoro. Strong wind is blowing outside although the night was clear. A good news — our unit (8 NLI) is not going to Peyun instead it is heard that we're moving to Punjab. I wish & pray that we move to Lahore (انشاءاللہ). NLI has been made a Regular Infantry Regiment. I plan to get myself posted permanently to 8 NLI as a parental officer. Allah make it good for me.

73rd Day in Baltoro Sector. The morning was not clear but around 1000 hrs the clouds vanished. We got the report that C-130 has taken-off from Rwp at 1100 hrs but it went back from the way as the clouds again covered the sky over Baltoro & snow fall started. So we sat back disappointed. Anyhow, in the evening weather again got clear. We pray that it remain clear tommorrow so we may get some ration & Aid for the Eid. انشاء

26 ۷ ذی الحجہ FRIDAY

۱۱ ذی الحجہ TUESDAY 30

77th day at Baltoro. Capt Adnan & Dr Sahib have departed for Urdukas. I along with Fida went to Pari-II & saw the loc for building another barrack there. Selected & marked the loc and came back. On the way back, I scored a duck. A tiring walk — four hrs one way.

3 April ١٥ ذي الحجة SUNDAY 4 / ١٤ ذي الحجة SATURDAY 3

81st day at Baltoro. Weather has suddenly got clear & Hel-msn is awaited. Reportedly, two Llamas are coming. Good for us. I got my Demand. Casualties evacuated.

87th day at Baltoro. My 90 days tenure at Baltoro is coming to an end, but It seems that I'll have to overstay my tenure as Capt Mudassar has been evacuated & Capt Aftab has been made to climb the Saddle again. Now Capt Adnan will relieve Capt Aftab & in turn he'll comedown & relieve me. Let's see when?

92nd day at Baltoro. A relatively clear day with high clouds & no wind. Anwar Shah & party brought some meat of Markhoor from the mountains. This one was hunted some days back & meat was stored in a cave under the snow. A delicious dinner is awaited.

24 Apr. Left Askoli for Apoligon at 0800 hrs. Reached Apoligon at 1500 hrs and had lunch there. At 1800 hrs, Maj Ateeq (New Zulu) came with his party on Toyota Pickup. On the same veh, I moved down & reached Dassu Base Camp at 1900 hrs. Stayed the ni.

۲۸ صفر SUNDAY 13 / ۲۷ صفر SATURDAY 12

12 June 99

My 27th birthday. At hamzigond, Maj Tariq & Capt Nabi Bukhsh are accompanying me. We enjoyed the sweets from home. A bad news – Comd 62 Bde Brig Nusrat Sial embraced Shahadat in Hel crash

13 June 99

Today, I am going to be inducted in Janvir Sec. At 1945 hrs, I moved to Gamokh on wheels & stayed the ni there. Capt Asim, Capt Mudassar, Lt Khalid & Lt Imran ex 5 NLI & Lt Shoeb

15 ۳۰ صفر TUESDAY

3rd day & I moved to Imtiaz with my party. Moved further on & reached Riaz Base, to releive Capt Qammar. Capt Qammar had captured Flight Lieutenant Nachikita of IAF. He showed me Nachi's eqpt & the reckage of the plane. We photographed as well.

Let's go-to war. ...

Early morning, Capt Qammar moved down to Imtiaz. At 1100 hrs, I got a call from Saddle that Badar has been bombarded and destroyed by Indian aircrafts. Maj Jawad (5NLI), Maj Ali (CS), Maj Zikrya (ISI), Capt Zulfiqar (CS) & Capt Izhar (5NLI) embrasfed Shahadat + Five other Jawans also. I along with 10 Jawans rushed to Badar to counter any possible enemy action. But en didn't dare. CO 5 NLI, doctor & Lt Khalid reached Badar soon by Hel and so I came back to Riaz after evac of cas.

19 SATURDAY/20 SUNDAY

19 June
7th day in the sector. We constructed another bunker but this time a larger one to accomodate a tent. Capt Sajid ex 5 NLI joined today on his way down. At 2130 hrs, I received orders for tommorow to move to Badar Base.

20 June. 8th day at Tanvir Sub Sector. I moved to Badar Base, reached there in $2\frac{1}{2}$ hrs — nice speed. Maj Inam & Lt Khalid (5NLI) were there. I got the orders to mov to Hassan.

13th day in the Sector. Kept constructing shell bunker th whole day. En Mirage-2000 bombers kept reccying the area, but didn't bomb. An SA-16 msl was fired on en a/c but it escaped. En shelling & rocketing kept on whole day. We are expecting 10-men party from Badar Base for rat & ammo dump. A news — 8 NLI is rel from Skardu & is coming to Jauver Sec, will be here within a week.

THURSDAY 1

19th day in sec. Lawar was attacked early morning but repulsed. At 1200 hrs Aqil was reported to be attacked. CO 5 NLI told me to go & cut off en route. I reccied the area & told him that en is behind Aqil Ridge & I can't leave my post vacant. So I didn't go.

(2) PAKISTAN'S ROLE IN FOSTERING TERRORISM IN KASHMIR: FACTS AND FIGURES*

Number of terrorist camps in Pakistan: 37

Number of terrorist camps in Pakistan-occupied Kashmir:49

Number of Pakistani-run terrorist camps in Afghanistan: 22

Total number of hardcore terrorists operating in Jammu and Kashmir: 2300

Total number of foreign mercenaries operating in Jammu and Kashmir: 900

Number of Pakistani terrorists killed by Indian forces: 291

---

* Source : Ministry of Home Affairs, New Delhi.

Number of Indian civilians killed by Pakistani terrorists: over 29,000

Number of firearms recovered from Pakistan-trained terrorists in India: 47,000

Amount of explosives recovered from Pakistan-trained terrorists in India; 60 tons (30,000 kg)

Number of explosions carried out by Pakistan-trained terrorists in India: 4,730

Nationalities of foreign mercenaries operating in Jammu and Kashmir: Pakistan, Pakistan-occupied Kashmir, Afghanistan, Egypt, Sudan, Yemen, Bahrain, Bangladesh, Iran, Iraq.

MAJOR PAKISTANI SUPPORTED TERRORIST GROUPS ACTIVE IN JAMMU AND KASHMIR:

1. Harkat ul-Ansar (renamed Harkat ul-Mujahideen) - Hqs: Muzaffarabad (Pakistan-Occupied Kashmir)
2. Lashkar-e-Tayyiba - Hqs: Muridke (Pakistan)

Number of people in Jammu and Kashmir killed in violence waged by Pakistan-supported terrorists over the last decade: over 20,000

Ethnic Cleansing in Kashmir: Nearly 300,000 Kashmiri Pandits (original Hindu inhabitants of Kashmir valley) driven out of their ancestral homeland by Pakistan-supported terrorists.

Pakistan's response to charges of terrorism support: "It only provides diplomatic and moral support to the terrorists". This is refuted in "credible reports of official Pakistani support of Kashmiri terrorist groups..." in the US State Department 1997 report on global terrorism. 70% of Pakistan's budget goes to support the military and debt servicing. A large portion of the military spending goes towards its operations in J & K including underwriting Kashmiri terrorists. (NY Times, Aug. 30, 1998, The Tribune, Oct 10, 1998).

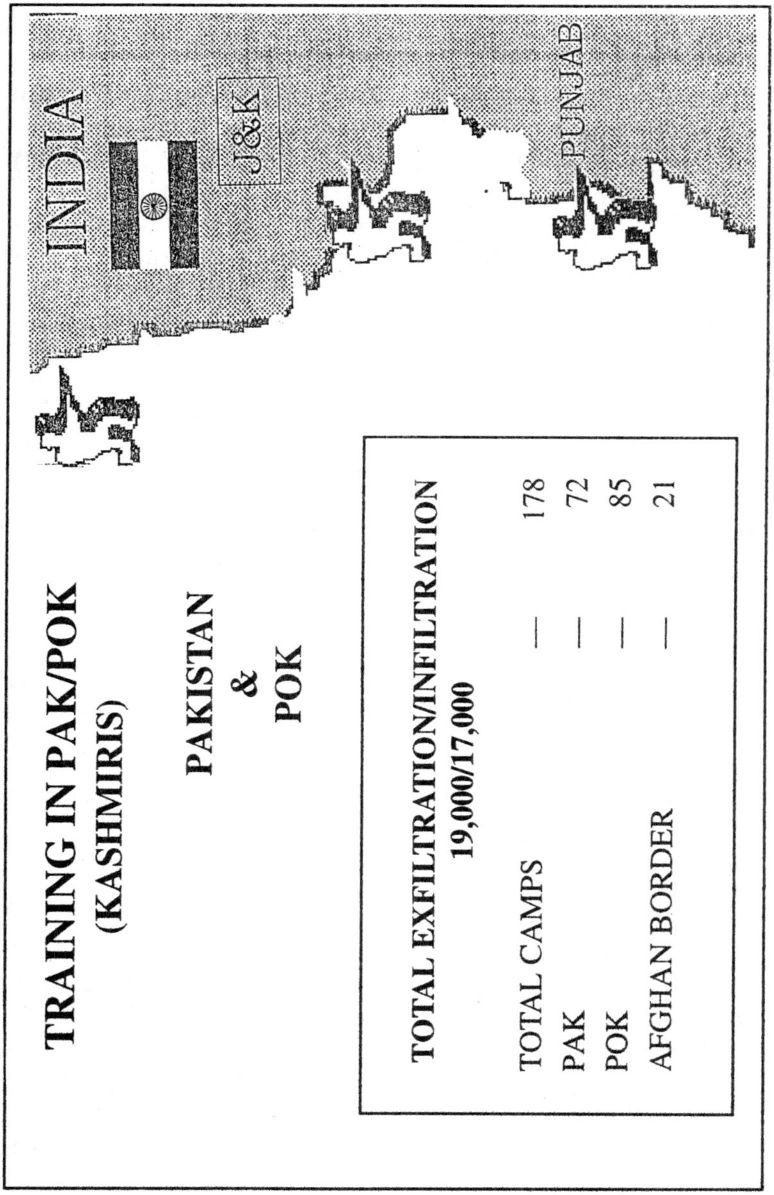
TRAINING IN PAK/POK
(KASHMIRIS)
PAKISTAN
&
POK
INDIA
J&K
PUNJAB
TOTAL EXFILTRATION/INFILTRATION
19,000/17,000
TOTAL CAMPS — 178
PAK — 72
POK — 85
AFGHAN BORDER — 21

TERRORIST ORGANISATIONS ACTIVE IN JAMMU AND KASHMIR

Al Faran-(Front organisation of Harkat ul-Ansar) - Al Jihad - LET -Lashkar-e-Tayyiba-(Hqs in Pakistan) - JuM -Jamiat-ul-Mujahideen - HuM -Hizb-ul-Mujahideen (Leadership in Pakistan) - MDA - Markaz-al-Dawa (Hqs in Pakistan) - HuA -Harkat ul-Ansar - IIM - Islami Inqulabi Mahaz - Bul - Bait-ul-Islam - AB - Al Barq - JKLF - Jammu and Kashmir Liberation Front (Amanullah Khan Faction, Hqs in Pakistan) - Ikhwan ul-Muslimeen - Hizbullha - Jaanbaaz Force - HKuM Harkat ul-Mujahideen - Jamiat-e-Islami - Allah Tigers - Tehrik ul-Mujahideen - Tehrik ul-Jehad-e-Islami - Pasdaran-e-Islam - Ansarullah

SOME OF THE MAJOR RECOVERIES

WEAPONS

1.	12.7 MM Anti Air Craft Machine Guns	-	04
2.	Heavy/Utility Machine Guns	-	46
3.	Rifles (G3/AK/Chinese/M-16/Sniper)	-	198
4.	Grenade/Rocket Launchers	-	19
5.	81/120 MM Mortars	-	12
6.	37 MM Twin Barrel AD Gun	-	01
7.	Stinger Missile with launcher	-	01
8.	23 MM Gun	-	01
9.	14.5 MM KPVT	-	01
10.	105 MM Howitzer less barrels	-	03
		Total	286

AMMUNITION

11.	Anti Personnel Mines	- 1406
12.	Artillery/Mortar Bombs	- 1200
13.	Chinese Rockets	- 32

(Plus large quantity of small arms ammunition, grenades and explosives amounting to approximately 35 tonnes).

EQUIPMENT AND CLOTHING

15.	Night vision device	- 06
16.	Communication sets (All types)	- 22
17.	Bullet proof jackets	- 17
18.	Gas masks	- 39
19.	Telephone cable	- 05 KMs
20.	Sleeping bags	- 33
21.	3-4 Men/Igloo tents	- 25

Note : Besides above, sizeable quantity of bunker construction material, Pak military literature, Pak currency, marked maps and personal items of Pak soldiers were also recovered.

EXTRACT OF SIMLA AGREEMENT PERTAINING TO LINE OF CONTROL

1 to 3. xxxxxxx.

4. In order to initiate the process of the establishment of durable peace, both the Government agree that :

(i) Indian and Pakistani forces shall be withdrawn to their side of the international border.

(ii) In Jammu and Kashmir, the line of control resulting from the cease-fire of December 17, 1971 shall be respected by both sides without prejudice to the recognized position of either side. Neither side shall seek to alter it unilaterally, irrespective of mutual differences and legal interpretations. *Both sides further undertake to refrain from the threat or the use of force in violation of this Line.*

(iii) The withdrawals shall commence upon entry into force of this Agreement and shall be completed within a period of 30 days thereof.

5. This Agreement will be subject to ratification by both countries in accordance with their respective constitutional procedures, and will come into force with effect from the date on which the Instruments of Ratification are exchanged.

6. Both Governments agree that their respective Heads will meet again at a mutually convenient time in the future and that, in the meanwhile, the representatives of the two sides will meet to discuss further the modalities and arrangements for the establishment of durable peace and normalisation of relations, including the questions of repatriation of prisoners of war and civilian internees, a final settlement of Jammu and Kashmir and the resumption of diplomatic relations.

Sd/-
(Indira Gandhi)
Prime Minister
Republic of India

Sd/-
(Zulfikar Ali Bhutto)
President
Islamic Republic of Pakistan

Simla, the 2nd July, 1972

C2: SLP

(3) INDO-PAK MILITARY BALANCE

The following is the line up of conventional military forces of Pakistan and India :

PAKISTAN

Army 520,000

9 Corps HQ • 2 armed div • 9 Corps arty bde • 19 inf div • 7 engr bde • 1 area comd (div) • 3 armd recce regt • 7 indep armd dbe • 1 SF gp (3bn) • 9 indep inf bde • 1 AD comd (3 AD gp: 8 bde)

INDIA

Army 980,000

HQ: 5 Regional Comd, 4 Fd Army, 11 Corps, 3 armed div (each 2-3 armd, 1 SP arty (2 SP fd, 1 med regt) bde) • 4 RAPID div (each 2 inf, 1 mech bde) • 18 inf div (each 2-5 inf, 1 arty bde

AVN 17 sqn
7 ac, 8 hel, 1 VIP, 1 obs flt

some have armd regt) •9 mtn div (each 3-4 bde, 1 or more arty regt) •1 arty div (3 bde) •15 Indep bde: 7 armd, 5 inf, 2 mtn, 1 AB/cdo •1 SSM regt (Privthi) •4 AD bde (plus 14 cadre) •3 engr bde.

EQUIPMENT

MBT 2, 120+: 15m-47, 345 M-48A5, 50 T-54/55,1,200 PRC Type-59, 250 PRC Type-69, 200+PRC Type-85, 100 T-80UD

APC 850 m-113

TOWED ARTY 1,590: 85MM: 200

PRC Type-56; 105mm: 300 M-101, 50 M-56 pack; 122 mm: 200 PRC Type-60, 400 PRC type-54; 130mm: 200 PRC Type-59-1; 155mm: 30 M-59, 60 M-114, 124 M-198; 203mm: 26 M-115

SP ARTY 240: 105mm: 50 M-7; 155mm: 150 M-109A2; 203mm; 40 M-110A2

MRL 122mm: 45 Azar (PRC Type-83)

EQUIPMENT

MBT est. 3,414 (est. 1,1,00 in store): some 700 T-55, est 1,500 T-72/-M1, 1,200 Vijayanta, est. 14 Arjun

LT TK 90 PT-76

RECCE 100 BRDM-2

AIFV 350 BMP- 1,1,00 BMP-2 (Sarath)

APC 157 OT-62/-64 (in store)

TOWED ARTY 1,175 (perhaps 600 in store) incl: 75mm: 900 75/24 mtn, FRY M-48; 105mm: some 1,300 IFG Mk I/II, 50 M-56; 122mm: some 550 D-30; 130mm: 750m-46; 155MM: 410 FH 77B

SP ARTY 105mm: 80 Abbot (30 in store); 130mm: 100 mod M-46 (70 in store)

MRL 122mm: 150 incl BM-21, LRAR; 214mm: Pinaka (being deployed)

MOR 81mm: 500; 120mm: 225

AM-50, M-61

SSM 18 Hatf 1, Hatf 2 (under development)

ATGW 800 incl: Cobra, 200 TOW (incl 24 on M-901 SP), Green Arrow (PRC Red Arrow
RL 89mm: M-20 3.5in

RCL 75mm : Type-52; 106mm; 35mm: 200 GDF-002; 37mm: PRC Type-55/-65; 40mm; M1, 100L60; 57mm: PRO Type-59

SAM 350 Stinger, Redeye, RBS-70, 500 Anza Mk-1/-2

MOR 81mm: L16A1; E1; 120mm: 500 Brandt

AM-50, E1; 160mm: 500 M-1943, 200 Tampella M-58 (150 in store)

SSM Prithvi (3-5 launchers)

ATGW Milan, AT-3 Sagger, AT-4 Spigot (some SP), AT-5 Spandrel (some SP)

RCL 57mm: 500 M-18; 84mm: Carl Gustav; 106mm: 1,000+ M-40A1
AD GUNS some 2,400: 20mm: Oerlikon (reported); 23mm: 300 ZU 23-2, 100 ZSU-23-4 SP; 30mm: 8 2S6 SP (reported); 40mm: 1,200 L40/60,800 L40/70

SAM 180
DEPLOYMENT
North 2 Corps with 8 inf, 2 mtn div West 3 Corps with 1 armd, 5 inf div, 3 RAPID Central 1 Corps with 1 armd, 1 RAPID East 3 Corps with 1 inf, 7 mtn div South 2 Corps with 1 armd, 3 inf div

Navy 22,000 (incl Naval Air 1,200 Marines and 2,000 Maritime Security Agency (See Paramilitary)	**Navy 55,000** (incl 7,000 Naval Aviation and 1,200 Marines, 2,000 women) **PRINCIPAL COMMAND** Western, Eastern, Southern, Far Eastern **SUB-COMMAND** Submarine, Naval Air
BASE Karachi (Fleet HQ)	**BASES** Mumbai (Bombay) (HQ Western Comd), Goa (HQ Naval Air), Karwar (under Construction), Kochi (Cochin) (HQ southern Comd), Visakhapatnam (HQ Eastern and submarines), Calcutta, Madras, Port Blair (Andaman Is (HQ Far Eastern comd), Arakonam (Naval Air) **FLEETS** Western base Bombay Eastern base Visakhapatnam
SUBMARINES 9 3 MG 110 SSI SF Midget sub-marines	**SUBMARINES** 19
PRINCIPAL SURFACE COMBATANTS 10	**PRINCIPAL SURFACE COMBATANTS** 25 **CARRIER** 1
DESTROYERS 2	**DESTROYERS** 6
FRIGATES 8	**FRIGATES** 18
COMBATANTS 10	**COMBATANTS** 49 **CORVETTES** 19
MISSILE CRAFT 5	**MISSILE CRAFT** 8
NAVAL AIR 7cbt ac, 12 armed hel	**NAVAL AVIATION** (5,000) 67 cbt ac, 83 armed hel Flying house some 180

ASW/MR 1 sqn with 4 Atlantic plus 3 in store, 3 P-3C (operated by Air Force)

ASW/SAR 2 hel sqn with 4 SA-319B (ASW), 6 Sea King Mk 45 (ASW), 2 Lynx HAS Mk-3 (ASW)

COMMS 3 Fokker F-27 ac (Air Force)

MARINES (1,200)

Air Force 45,000
FGA 7 sqn
FTR 10 sqn
RECCE 1 sqn with 12 Mirage IIIRP
ASW/MR 1 sqn with 4 Atlantic, 3 P3C
SAR 1 hel sqn with 6 SA-319

TRANSPORT 12
MISSILES

ATTACK 2 sqn with 17 Sea Harrier FRS Mk-51, 2 T-60 trg

ASW 6 hel sqn with 26 Chetak, 7 Ka-25, 18, 32 Sea King Mk 42A/B

AEW 3 Ka-31
MR 3 sqn with 5 Il-38, 8 Tu-142m Bear F, 20 Do-228, 15 BN-2 Defender

COMMS 1 sqn will ac BN-2 Islander, 10 do-228 hel 3 Chetak
MISSILES
AAM R-550 Magic I and II

ASM Sea Eagle, sea Skua
MARINES (1,200)

Air Force 140,000
FGA 17 sqn
FTR 20 sqn
ECM 4 Canberra B (1) 58 (ECM/target towing, plus 2 Canberra TT-18 target towing)
ELINT 2 Boeing 707, 2 Boeing 737
AEW 4 HS-748
TANKER 6 1L-78
MARITIME ATTACK 6
ATTACK HEL 3 sqn with 32 Mi-25
RECCE 2 sqn
MR/SURVEY 2
TRANSPORT 12 sqn
MISSILES

ASM AM-39 Exocet, AGM-65 Maverick

AAM AIM-7 Sparrow, AIM-9 Sidewinder, R-530, R-550 Magic

SAM 7 bty
6 each with 24 Crotale, 1 with 6 CSA-1 (SA-2)

Paramilitary 247,000 active
NATIONAL GUARD 185,000

FRONTIER CORPS (Ministry of Interior) 35,000
11 regt (40bn), 1 indep armd car sqn; 45 UR-416 APC
PAKISTAN RANGERS 25,000
MARITIME SECURITY AGENCY
2,000
1 Alamgir (US Gearing DD) (no ASROC or TT), 4 Barakat PCC, 4 (PRC Shsnghai) PFI

ASM AS-7 Kerry, AS-11B (ATGW), AS-12, AS-30, Sea Eagle, AM 39 Exct, AS-17 Krypton

AAM AA-7 Ape, AA-8 Aphid, AA-10 Alamo,
AA-11 Archer, R-550 Magic, super 530D

SAM 38 sqn with 280 Divina V75SM/VK (SA-2), Pechora (SA-3), SA-5, SA-10

Paramilitary 1,090,000 active
NATIONAL SECURITY GUARDS 7,400
SPECIAL PROTECTION GROUP 3,000
SPECIAL FRONTIER FORCE 9,000
RASHTRIYA RIFLES 40,000
DEFENCE SECURITY CORPS 31,000
INDO-TIBETAN BORDER POLICE 32,200
ASSAM RIFLES 52,500
RAILWAY PROTECTION FORCE 70,000
CENTRAL INDUSTRIAL SECURITY FORCE 88,600
CENTRAL RESERVE POLICE FORCE 165,300
BORDER SECURITY FORCE 185,000
HOME GUARD (R) 472,000

STATE ARMED POLICE 400,000

CIVIL DEFENCE 394,000 (R)

COAST GUARD some 23 PFI, PLUS BOATS

COAST GUARD over 6,000

PATROL CRAFT 35

Source : Military Balance, London

(4) POLITICAL AND CONSTITUTIONAL DEVELOPMENTS IN J & K SINCE 1947

S. No.	Events	Date/Year
1.	Invasion of J &K by tribal hordes from Pakistan	Oct. 23, 1947
2.	"Instrument of Accession" signed by Maharaja in favour of India	Oct. 26, 1947
3.	"Instrument of Accession" accepted by Governor General	Oct. 26, 1947
4.	Sheikh Abdullah appointed emergency administrator	Oct. 26, 1947
5.	Indian troops land in Kashmir	Oct. 27, 1947
6.	India refers Kashmir issue to the U. N. Security Council	Jan. 01, 1948
7.	India & Pakistan called upon to take measures to improve the situation and to inform about any material change in it	Jan. 17, 1948
8.	3- Members U. N. Commission for India & Pakistan (UNCIP) set up	Jan. 20, 1948
9.	Membership of UNCIP raised to five	Apr. 21, 1948
10.	Emergency administration replaced by interim Govt. headed by Sheikh Abdullah	March 5, 1948.
11.	UNCIP resolution providing for : Cease fire	Aug. 13, 1948
	: withdrawal of Pak troops & all outsiders followed by reduction of Indian forces	
	: Determination of the future status of J & K in accordance with the "Will of the people"	
12.	Ceasfire proclaimed under UN auspices.	Jan 01, 1949.
13.	UNCIP resolution reiterating resolution 13 Aug. 1948 and providing for appointment of plebiscite administrator by Secretary General	Jan. 05, 1949

S. No.	Events	Date/Year
14.	All J & K National Conference passed a resolution for convening a constituent assembly based on adult suffrage for the purpose inter alia of determining the future shape & affiliation of the state of J& K including the issue of accession of India, & to frame a Constitution for the state	Oct. 27, 1950
15.	Elections for the constituent assembly held & assembly formed. All 75 seats won by the National Conference. The Praja Parishad, a Jammu based political party, wanting complete accession to India had boycotted the election.	Aug-Sept. 1951
16.	Discussions between Govt. of India & Kashmir leaders resulted in what is known as "Delhi Agreement". It indicated the dynamic nature of constitutional relationship between the state of J & K the Indian union & reaffirmed accession of state of Indian Union.	July 24, 1952
17.	J & K constitution adopted by the state constituent assembly.	Nov. 17, 1956
18.	J & K constitution came into effect	Jan. 26, 1957
19.	Election to the J & K legislative assembly held (NC won 68 out of 75 seats).	March, 1957
20.	State assembly unanimously decided to seek amendment of the state constitution to provide for extension of the jurisdiction of the election commission of India and the Supreme Court over the J & K state.	1959
21.	General election in J & K held (NC got 70 seats, others-5)	1962
22.	Holy Relic stolen from Hazratbal shrine Srinagar, massive agitation started by an action committee under the leadership of Maulvi Farooq.	Dec. 27,1963
23.	Infiltration of intruders followed by attack by Pakistan on J & K and its repulsion by Indian Army.	August, 1965
24.	Tashkent agreement signed between India and Pakistan.	Jan. 10, 1966
25.	Assembly election 1967 (Cong-61, NC-8, others-6)	Mar 5-6, 1967
26.	Assembly election 1972 JEI participated in elections for the first time (Cong-58, JEI-5, others-12)	Feb. 08, 1972
27.	India & Pakistan sign Shimla Agreement, agreed that issues between them to be settled bilaterally. Agreement supercedes all previous pronouncements on Kashmir. Ceasefire line converted into LOC.	July 03, 1972
28.	Kashmir accord concluded. Indian Prime Minister said "Clock cannot be put back". On behalf of Kashmiri leadership it was reiterated that "Accession of the state of J & K to India is not a matter in issue"	February, 1975
29.	Sheikh Abdullah became Chief Minister. Plebiscite front was found and merged with National Conference.	July 9, 1975
30.	Assembly elections held. NC won 46 out of 75 seats, JEI-1 seat (68 percent voter turnout).	July 3, 1977

S. No.	Events	Date/Year
31.	J & K Islami Jamat-E-Tulba formed. Founder member Dr. Ayub Thukar, now based in London-promotes pro-Pak fundamentalist militant ideology -receives support from Pakistan.	Sept. 1977
32.	J & K Mahaz-E-Azahi formed. It's leader Azam In quilabi now in Pakistan	1977-78
33.	Sheikh Abdullah passes away & Dr. Farooq Abdullah sworn in as Chief Minister.	Sept. 8, 1982
34.	J & K assembly elections held. NC won 46 out of 75 seats. (73.5% voter turn out)	June, 1983
35.	Dr. Farooq Abdullah forms Govt.	June 12, 1983
36.	Governor's Rule imposed. Followed by President's Rule after large scale communal violence.	Sept. 6, 1986
37.	Coalition Government (Cong-I/NCF) formed	Nov. 7, 1986
38.	State assembly elections held. Cong-I NCF alliance secured 66 out of 76 seats. Complaints/allegations of rigging.	March. 1987
39.	NCF-Congress-I coalition Government formed.	March 23, 1987
40.	Sporadic violence and protests in valley, large scale exfiltration/infiltration across he LOC culminating in large scale civil disturbances in early 1990	August 1988-90
41.	Parliamentary elections held. Only 5% voter turn-out due to boycott call and threats by militants	November, 1989
42.	State Government resigns and state brought under Governor's rule.	January 19, 1990
43.	President's rule promulagated in the state.	July 18, 1990
44.	Charar-e-Sharief Shrine burnt by militants.	May 10-11, 1995
45.	Armed militants enter Hazrat Bal Shrine; Shrine peacefully vacated by militants; encounter of police with militants (32 militants and one police personnel killed in the episode-damage to Shrine/Relic prevented).	May 24-30, 1996
46.	Lok Sabha elections held. Cong-1 won 4 seats and BJP & JD, 1 each. NC did not participate. Voter turnout-41-83%	May, 1996
47.	Decision of Central Executive Committee of NCF to participate in Assembly Elections	Aug. 1996
48.	Notification by Election Commission issued for Assembly Elections in J & K in 4 phases	Aug./Sep. 1996
49.	Revocation of President's Rule and formation of newly elected Govt.	Oct. 9, 1996
50.	State Human Rights Commission Bill passed by J & K State Assembly.	April 30, 1997
51.	General Elections to the Lok Sabha held along with rest of the country	1998
52.	General Elections to the Lok Saha held along with rest of the country	1999

Give below are some data related to Pakistan supported errorist activities in Jammu and Kashmir. The statistics have een prepared by the Indian Ministry of Home Affairs :

Terrorist Violence in J & K

	Total incidents	*Attacks on SF**	*Attacks on other*	*Abuduction***	*Explosion and arson*	*Other incidents*
988	390	6	1	—	142	241
989	2154	49	73	2	840	1192
990	3905	1098	485	57	1810	512
991	3122	1999	321	100	611	191
992	4971	3413	507	124	744	307
993	4457	2573	539	181	900	445
994	6895	2675	1594	332	1774	852
995	6819	2570	1836	395	1633	780
996	5523	1473	2133	473	1260	657
997	3421	1212	1399	448	672	457
998 (June)	1213	458	505	141	256	20
otal	42870	17526	9393	2255	10642	5654

* SF Includes Army, BSF, ITBP, CRPF & JKP

** Also included in attacks on others

Death Toll in Terrorist Violence

	1988-91	*1992*	*1993*	*1994*	*1995*	*1996*	*1997*	*1998 June*	*Total*
otal illed	2693	1909	2567	2867	2768	2858	2199	831	18691
F	331	187	216	199	234	185	186	85	1613
iovt fficials	123	36	34	26	46	67	26	8	366
olitical eaders & ctivists	37	4	8	6	12	29	20	5	121
udiciary	5	—	1	—	2	2	—	—	10
ress/Media	3	1	1	2	2	1	—	—	10
eligious eaders	4	1	—	1	2	1	1	—	10
oreigners	1	—	—	1	1	—	—	—	3
ilitants	798	873	1330	1596	1332	1209	1075	310	8523

Kidnappings by Militants

	1990-93	*1994*	*1995*	*1996*	*1997*	*1998 (June)*	*Tota*
Incidents	462	332	395	473	448	141	225
Persons Abducted	681	368	548	666	440	148	285
Foreigners*	12	2	6	—	—	—	2
Political Activists	116	3	3	4	3	—	12
Judiciary	1	—	—	—	—	—	
Religious Leaders	2	1	2	—	—	—	
Other Professionals	13	3	—	1	—	—	1
Press/Media (Attack/Kidnappings etc.)	13	6	3	1	—	—	2
Govt. Officers	128	36	55	48	39	2	30
Killed	188	157	207	345	164	56	111
Released**	346	164	163	104	82	21	87
Whereabout Not Known	—	—	—	—	—	88	8

* Israelis-7, Swedish-2, Dutch-1, Japanese-1, French-1, British-4, Norwegiar 1, German-1, US-2, Nepalese-8 (Besides British 3, US 1 from and nea Delhi)

** Released after extortion, torture, exchange of militants etc.

Attacks on Minorities

	1990-92	*1993*	*1994*	*1995*	*1996*	*1997*	*199 Jun*
Hindus Killed	289	87	95	97	89	68	10
Sikhs Killed	26	7	5	4	2	1	–

Migration of Minorities from Valley to other parts of Country

Place	*Number of Families*
Jammu	28,561
Delhi	19,338
Others	2,347
Total	50,248

The Indian government is spending around Rs. 400 million per annum o their relief in addition to providing other support.

Recovery of Weapons/Communication Equipment

Weapons/Explosives	*1988-94*	*1995*	*1996*	*1997*	*1998 (June)*	*Total*
Rocket Launchers	581	36	43	81	94	835
Machine Guns	781	81	96	76	26	1060
Ak Series Rifles	12471	2055	2150	1725	590	18991
Sniper Rifles	118	38	49	60	26	292
Mortar	19	12	3	3	51	88
Grenade Launchers	67	27	21	98	30	243
Pistol/Revolvers	4353	965	1052	1024	313	7655
Ammunition (Assorted in lacs)	18.34	3.42	3.43	2.70	1.47	29.03
Grenades	15449	2870	3949	5124	2361	29753
Rockets	1535	170	378	479	277	2839
Rocket Booster	668	24	119	208	72	1091
Mines	3440	634	552	408	404	5579
Guns	508	370	303	191	61	1433
Explosives (KG)	7607	1484	2382	6448	1352	18173
Bombs	1440	126	31	204	80	1881
WT Sets	509	246	413	302	233	1703

INDEX